WILLIAM HOLDEN

WILLIAM HOLDEN

A Pyramid Illustrated History of the Movies

by
WILL HOLTZMAN

General Editor: **TED SENNETT**

**PUBLICATIONS
NEW YORK**

WILLIAM HOLDEN
A Pyramid Illustrated History of the Movies

A PYRAMID BOOK

Copyright © 1976 by Pyramid Communications, Inc.

All rights reserved. No part of this publication may be reproduced or transmitted in any form or by any means, electronic or mechanical, including photocopy, recording, or any information storage and retrieval system, without permission in writing from the publisher.

Pyramid edition published August 1976

Library of Congress Catalog Card Number: 76-23510

Printed in the United States of America

Pyramid Books are published by Pyramid Publications (Harcourt Brace Jovanovich). Its trademarks, consisting of the word "Pyramid" and the portrayal of a pyramid, are registered in the United States Patent Office.

PYRAMID PUBLICATIONS
(Harcourt Brace Jovanovich)
757 Third Avenue, New York, N.Y. 10017

graphic design by anthony basile

ACKNOWLEDGMENTS

For starters, many thanks to my parents, Don and Ev, for being my first and best teachers, and to Linda and Gene for their part in keeping, as Katharine Hepburn would say, "insanity in the family."

For moral support and friendship, I am grateful to: Dana Asbury, Louise Beach, Victoria Bijur, Randy and Joan Covitz, Richard Hunt, Bill Pearson, Maizie Ragan, Brian Skarstad, Kathy Sulkes, and Frank Trechsel. Thanks to Nate and Pat Pearson for a generous boost.

My gratitude to Rod Bladel and the staff of the Research Division of the Lincoln Center Library, and to the entire staff of the Motion Picture Section of the Library of Congress, for running a public gold mine.

I am indebted to Gary Collins for his generosity in obtaining films, and to Steve Ross for using me as a test case (and for beating me regularly at poker). Rhonda Bloom has been a tireless source and a valued friend throughout.

Thanks to Rich Slotkin for putting me on the scent years ago (and for employment in lean times), and especially to my editor, Ted Sennett, for his love of film and the long shot.

Very special thanks to Sylvia Shepard for being my spiritual mainstay and number one critic, and to Pearl, for running a close second.

My greatest debt of thanks is to Jeanine Basinger—mentor, guardian angel, and unswerving friend, to whom I plan to erect a statue after my first million. Thanks, also, to John and Savannah for being good buddies and generous with Jeanine.

A final nod to Harpo and Susan Marx, for inspiration.

Photographs: Jerry Vermilye. The Memory Shop, Movie Star News, Cinemabilia, and the companies that produced and distributed the films of William Holden.

CONTENTS

The Scenario: Never Beholden	11
...And Turn Left at Pasadena	16
Gilded, But Not Giddy	25
A Star is Bored	35
The War Ends, The Battle Begins	54
Apple Pie Gone Awry	73
Paving the Road to Kwai	96
The Holden Grail	121
Full Circle	144
Bibliography	147
The Films of William Holden	148
Index	155

As Big Davey Harvey in
RACHEL AND THE STRANGER (1948)

"I didn't ask for any of this. None of it at all." — William Holden to *The New York Times,* December, 1965

THE SCENARIO: NEVER BEHOLDEN

There is no William Holden, only William Holden films. Among studio executives, that's known as eclipsed star power. Among others, that's known as acting.

Not that Holden was ever a box-office drain. In the fifties, when television threatened to bring the film industry to its knees, he was working more than ever and paying the studio bills. But Holden was never a sacred image, and was rarely predictable. He had no tricks or trademarks to tote from picture to picture as an instant index to his character. He was a half generation off pace, too late for the studio-spawned superstars, too early for the stage-trained method actors.

So Holden followed his instincts, battled typecasting, and hit upon a blend of technique and repertoire that sired several of the finest performances in motion picture history. Joe Gillis of *Sunset Boulevard,* Sergeant Sefton of *Stalag 17,* Hal Carter of *Picnic,* Pike Bishop of *The Wild Bunch* —the only thing they had in common was that they had nothing in common. For Holden had no concrete star's image to protect, no character tradition to uphold. The part was the thing, and he was able to tap a wide range of gestures, emotions, and faces in its interest, though never at the price of theatricality. Film was his medium from the first and he knew its boundaries implicitly. He was always a credit to a strong director and he approached his work with the canny professionalism of a man who had not chosen acting, but had been chosen by it.

In 1938 at the invitation of a talent scout, William Holden stepped off a junior college stage and onto a Hollywood backlot. Within months he made his debut in the prestigious *Golden Boy* and in the next thirty-seven years added some sixty starring roles, an Oscar, and a television Emmy. But he was never counting, and he never looked over his shoulder. The past seemed remote beyond measure.

Long before there was William Holden the movie actor, there was Bill Beedle the church-going, knee-scraping nubbin from O'Fallon, Illinois. The Beedle family moved to California, Bill grew, and the rough edges rounded. There was nothing extraordinary in his looks or manner, unless it was an intense ordinariness. He was of average height and build, sturdily athletic,

As Sefton in STALAG 17 (1953)

and possessed of a boyishly handsome face with an easy, crescent smile.

To the Paramount agent who later signed him, Bill seemed at a glance the prototype of the boy next door. But under the eventual scrutiny of the screen, he betrayed a veiled, multi-layered mystique. There was a tension in him, a complex man trying to break through a complacent mask, and that is what riveted audiences for three decades—the feeling that they were witnessing the real, not the ideal, and that through his dramatic growth they might learn about their own reality.

Those who have written off Holden as the Hollywood Everyman have been blind to his dramatic grain, or simply naive. He was a subtle grid of post-war man, fallible and mortal. He did not go charging off to death, tunic flapping, sword aloft. He did not swagger into a dusty showdown with a six-gun and a slogan. His heroism was tempered, his valor discrete. For him, sacrifice was often born of coercion, or the split-second impulse of desperation. He doubted, he flinched, and sometimes wept, and often he died, falling without false grandeur.

Holden's non-dramatic work was likewise edged. As a light comedian or farceur, he had ability but no flare. His forte was hard, blistering humor, cynicism with a snicker. As a leading man or heartthrob, he lacked splash or dash, but won a staunch following with a sex appeal accentuated through understatement. As a period player, he was effortlessly authentic, with just a tinge of modernity to avoid the quaint or antique.

And tucked away in each character was a portion of William Holden, seldom large enough for quick identification, usually small enough to be overlooked. It is only through watching a number of his films that a composite of the man emerges. He was a shy, interior person, moody and volatile, capable of kindness and cruelty. In public life, he was fire and water, a quick-tempered, hard-drinking individualist, a politically conservative, civic-minded family man.

It was years before Hollywood put together the pieces and saw him as a sensitive, intelligent, and gifted actor, but by then it was too late. Holden owned Holden, owed nothing to the studios, and treated Hollywood as cavalierly as it had treated him. While the press puzzled over the change and haggled over his debt to fans, Holden kept growing and experimenting beyond what acting had to offer him. He became a businessman, then a devoted conservationist, acting only as it financed other interests. Hollywood had taken the art out of acting for him, and if dollars and cents were what was left, then he would have his share. Holden was shrewd and gutsy enough to beat the industry at its own game, and the industry never really forgave him.

Holden's own disaffection ran deeper than even he cared to admit. He was in the fifties vanguard of entertainment expatriates who migrated to Switzerland, and once he was in motion, he never slowed. It wasn't certain if Holden was fox or hound, but the chase always seemed of life and death moment. In many ways, he was his own worst enemy, as he once explained, "I don't really know why, but danger has always been an important thing in my life—to see how far I could lean without falling, how fast I could go without cracking up." He pressed limits that have sent others reeling.

With his far-flung business and acting commitments, Holden became a truly international figure, and it was nearly two decades before he again turned to California as someplace other than a quick stop and a bad memory.

Today, William Holden lives secluded near Palm Springs. Both he and Hollywood are older, each having surmounted a middle-age hump. Holden is a vibrant fifty-eight with an undiminished acting talent and a face that looks its age. As he begins his thirty-eighth year in motion pictures, he may be musing over a career renaissance, wondering whether Hollywood might once again "discover" him, a fluent, veteran actor in its midst. But if he were to recall a small midwestern town, lost simplicity, and the cost of celebrity, it's just possible he would decline the favor.

As Sears in THE BRIDGE ON THE RIVER KWAI *(1957)*

"I know I'm not exactly dry behind the ears yet and have everything to learn, but I figure if I keep working as hard as I can and trying as hard as I can, maybe I'll get along all right."—to Screen Book, July, 1939

... AND TURN LEFT AT PASADENA

In the early spring of 1922, the Beedle family of O'Fallon picked up bag and baggage and packed off to Pasadena, California. For William Franklin Beedle, Sr., it meant leaving a job as a druggist and hiring on as an industrial chemist at the George W. Gooch Laboratories. For Mrs. Mary Beedle, it meant interrupting her career as a school teacher. For three-year-old Bill, Jr., (born April 17, 1918) it all meant very little at the time. None of the Beedles gave second thought to the fact that they were moving into the primary orbit of that newest of synthetic Southern Californian fixtures, Hollywood.

There was little reason to. Middle-class respectability had always been a shield against vulgarity, and the Beedles were nothing if not middle-class. William, Sr., a model of upward mobility, quickly became Gooch's top chemical and fertilizer analyst. This enabled his wife, then teaching in the Pasadena and Monrovia School systems, to set aside work and ride herd on the Beedle boys (now numbering three with the births of Bob and Richard), nudging them into church and out of trouble as fit the occasion.

The boys seldom gave her cause for concern. Even spunky Bill, Jr. croaked away merrily and willingly each Sunday in the Oneonta Congregationalist Church Choir. And if he was no Einstein, neither did anyone have to burn down the school house to get him out of Wild Rose Grammar School. As a matter of fact, Bill landed the lead in the sixth-grade production of *Rip Van Winkle,* garnering the usual critical acclaim awarded ten-year-olds who speak their lines loudly and don't bump into the scenery.

But this was not a particularly stage-struck Winkle. Bill was more diligent at perpetrating the garden variety of boyhood vices. Whatever danger this tranquil community did not provide, he gladly invented: tottering along the handrail of a certain "suicide" bridge, or leaping from a standing position over a four-and-a-half foot wrought-iron fence against the wagers of pals who were willing to risk their nickels on the off chance that he

Around 1940

An early publicity portrait

might skewer himself on the top spikes.

Bill never missed. His father, a fine amateur gymnast at McKendree College in Illinois, had taken care to school his sons in the virtues of acrobatics. With Bill, it was always the challenge of objects and obstacles and rarely the scuffling of most scrappy kids. The fact that he managed to parlay this into ready pocket money was, for him, just a practical equation.

Where Mr. Beedle fared less well was in implanting the rewards of a career in industrial chemistry. Here, it was not a question of aptitude but of attitude, and Bill loathed his chemistry studies. Successive summers spent taking core samples of guano and other high-yield fertilizer, aboard ships in Los Angeles harbor, did nothing to improve his outlook.

Yet short of an adolescent crush on motorcycles and a fleeting desire to ride with the then popular Victor McLaglen Motorcycle Daredevils, he had no secret ambition. Responsible but restless, Bill was willing to let the proper course present itself in due time. Until then, it might as well be chemistry as anything.

But no alternative was forthcoming, partly because Bill shouldered none of the career imperatives common among needier families. The Beedles met with a minimum of hardship during the Depression years, and what little they encountered came more as a result of family health problems than the rampant economic ills. Even during the mid-thirties, when William, Sr. was bedridden with pneumosilicosis, Mary Beedle was able to resume teaching, offsetting what in other families might have meant despair and disintegration. During these cushioned hard times, young Bill readily stepped into the role of man of the house, lightening his mother's load and strengthening an already sturdy family bond.

By the time Senior was on his feet again, Junior had ripened from a boy without direction to a young man without direction. All the same, upon graduating from South Pasadena High School in 1936, Bill immediately enrolled at South Pasadena Junior College as a chemistry major. His parents were elated but, as Bill would admit years later, he had absolutely no wish to succeed his father at the Gooch Laboratories. For one, that field held no allure for him, but more important, the old restlessness was still there.

After a year of chafing under his chosen curriculum, Bill suspended his schooling for some hoboing in the style of middle-class suburbia. Bill rounded up a good friend, a durable Plymouth, and the wherewithal, and set off on a half-year's pilgrimage that wound up a continent's breadth away in New York City. He was bedazzled. The hum of big city life seemed better attuned to Bill's own meter and appetite for excitement. It certainly did more to feed his imagination than had the humdrum of small town life.

By 1939, New York had regained much of its former vitality. With the worst of the Depression over, people were once more finding stage entertainment affordable, and, with vaudeville moldering in the grave, the theater world became the ready pulse of regeneration. Not only were the seasoned talents returned to form, but a host of WPA-nursed newcomers were now set loose on the larger theatrical scene. Soon after Bill, friend, and jalopy hit town, a play opened at the Belasco Theater under the general auspices of the Group Theater from the pen of that organization's favorite son, Clifford Odets. *Golden Boy* won cheers and soon settled in for a long run. While Bill missed seeing it, he hungrily took in most of the other current shows. True to the maxim, the native Illinoisan was stagestruck, vowing to return to New York after college and devote himself to acting. It may not have been a blood pact, but it was the first hint of career commitment.

When Bill returned to school the next fall, he resumed his chemistry toils grudgingly, but as a personal concession, added a course in radio drama. It wasn't long before the new passion began to cramp the supposed profession. Soon Bill was performing in radio plays for the local station, KECA, as the withered science ties eroded further.

If Bill's radio work provided a first brush with acting, it was left to a friend to give the final push toward the stage. Among Bill's radio cohorts was a young theatrical triple threat named Bob Ben Ali, who wrote, directed and produced plays at South Pasadena Junior College. It was Bob who first suggested that Bill come out from behind the microphone and sample the stage. Hesitant over his shyness and lack of experience, Bill demurred. Bob persisted. He had completed a play about Marie Curie entitled *Manya* and Bill would be a wonderful asset to the production. Still "no." But there was an ideal part, Marie's eighty-year-old father-in-law, Eugene. All it asked was a tolerance for make-up and a knack for geriatric voicemanship. Bill finally agreed to join the cast as a personal favor, but only for a limited run.

Manya went into rehearsal with the regulars of the Pasadena Workshop Theater, and one erstwhile chemist. The play opened in late spring and completed a

successful stint, as Bill Beedle hobbled and hemmed his way through the role like a trouper. After all, his last stage appearance had been as the 120-year-old Winkle; he could play down to his part. Toward the end of the play's scheduled run, there occurred the first of a peculiar series of events that was to deposit Bill some distance from a junior college stage.

Gilmore Brown, managing director of the Pasadena Community Playhouse, dropped in on *Manya* one evening and was sufficiently impressed with the workmanlike production to invite the cast to extend the run for an additional ten nights at his Playbox Theater. Among other things, the Playbox served as a showcase for local talent and was known to have launched the careers of many movie personalities. The ardent thespians of the troupe lunged at the offer. Bill went along for the ride.

Always willing to sift for talent in his own backyard, Paramount Pictures' chief talent scout, Artie Johnson, got wind of the extension and, on a tip, dispatched an assistant, Milton Lewis, to reconnoiter the play's female lead. Lewis attended the first performance and clearly liked what he saw. Ever ready to gamble an audition on a prospective star, he not only offered the actress a screen test, but invited two other cast members to come along. One, a supporting actress, was beside herself with elation. The other, that winsome amateur straining to look and sound four times his age, was flattered but his feet never left the ground. Bill Beedle explained that he would be unavailable for the screen test due to more pressing tests of his own, chemistry, to be exact. Astounded that, for once, someone had refused to rise to the bait, Lewis departed and passed on the story to his boss back at Paramount. Johnson was amused by the rare show of good sense and instructed Lewis to invite the young chemist to visit the studio after exams.

It was June before Bill dropped in but he was promptly assigned to a test. As an economy measure, he shared his screen time with an attractive young stock actress named Rebecca Wasson. From all reports, this, his first whiskerless turn, was dismal. But the test showed something more: an engaging, casual smile; a natural, athletic body; a relaxed manner; and the rare, fresh-faced good looks that were short of debilitating glamour while far from the homogenized handsomeness of so many Hollywood hopefuls. One thing was certain: actors were a dime a dozen in Hollywood; faces were always worth a second look. Paramount signed him for the lavish sum of $50 per week. Just like that, he was in

—or so it seemed.

Bill finally shook off his doubts and warmed to the idea of serious acting—a crucial error at that juncture. The lot of the studio bit player was anything but dramatically fulfilling. In his first outing, Bill sledged rocks in a programmer called *Prison Farm*. His next time out found him delivering his first line, "Thank you," along with ninety-nine others in a graduation scene from *Million Dollar Legs*. Prospects did not improve noticeably, even after Bill was selected for a Paramount unit known as the "Golden Circle," a brace of fledglings meant to serve the dual purposes of studio image troupe and, at some remove, as a talent incubator. The "Circle" numbered twelve and included Ellen Drew, Susan Hayward, Betty Field, Robert Preston, plus a handful of lesser lights destined for the ranks of Hollywood castoffs, although at the time, Bill didn't seem especially safe from oblivion. The balance of 1938 brought him no more than a string of promotional tours and a new name, both courtesy of Terry De Lapp, head of Paramount's publicity department.

Concerned that Beedle gave the unsavory impression of insects, De Lapp called Bill to his office for the ritual Hollywood renaming. When Bill arrived, the publicist was on the telephone to good friend and associate editor of the *Los Angeles Times,* William Holden. De Lapp figured this was a lucky shortcut and asked the two if they would mind sharing the same name. There were no objections as Beedle became Holden.

As his first calendar year in Hollywood drew to a close, Bill took stock in his career to date, and wondered whether, if worse came to worse, the Gooch Laboratories might still have a spot for a slightly used actor with a borrowed name.

GILDED, BUT NOT GIDDY

> *"Don't tell me about movie people being a jealous, self-centered, backstabbing bunch. Anything I know about acting I've learned from other actors."*
> —to *Colliers*, June, 1951

There have been nearly as many paths to stardom as stars. Yet in the studio clover days of the thirties and forties, the movie industry acquired an almost smothering fondness for the "discovery," also known as the "find" and the "overnight sensation." Here was a delectably serviceable motif which celebrated the moguls as keen-eyed impresarios, touted the directors as agile molders of the roughhewn and above all affirmed the worn notion that celebrity was at heart a democratic phenomenon, one which might be conferred upon most anyone. If, in fact, the "overnight" sometimes meant years or was spent on a casting-couch, the studios paid no heed. On word from above, any publicity hack could refurbish the facts and confirm the ethic, that Hollywood was still the place of dreams.

In the early spring of 1939, the only dreams Columbia Pictures' president Harry Cohn was having were bad ones—he had secured a tailor-made starring vehicle and could find no star. Earlier that year, he had purchased the film rights to Clifford Odets' provocative melodrama, *Golden Boy,* which had just completed a resounding Broadway run. The ordinarily frugal Cohn had bid a goodly $75,000 for the property, with an eye towards Warner Brothers' John Garfield (who played a supporting role in the stage version) in the featured part of Joe Bonaparte. What the Columbia executive unaccountably failed to foresee was the fitful squabbling of rival studios, and 1939 found him on the outs with his Warner Brothers counterpart, Jack Warner. Cohn had gotten the play, but not the actor.

Turning thumbs down on Luther Adler, who originated the part for the Group Theater, Cohn let the selection of a lead slide and began to assemble the rest of the production. Rouben Mamoulian was chosen to direct and, in quick succession, the major roles were handed over to screen veterans Barbara Stanwyck and Adolphe Menjou, and stage imports Lee J. Cobb and Sam Levene. Things were beginning to take on the gloss of Hollywood respectability, making the thorny absence of a lead all the more exasperating.

Hoping to turn the dilemma to advantage, Columbia publicists concocted a nationwide talent hunt for Joe Bonaparte, meant to drum up free press for the picture before a probable return to the studio stables for one of the usual contract players. Elsewhere, even Mamoulian helped spread the honey and feed the growing mystique. In no uncertain terms, he told the wire services, "The picture industry will gain a new and vital personality out of *Golden Boy*. The result can't help but create a new film star."

Responses poured in from every nook of the country. Everyone from legitimate actors to dishwashers was sending in resumés and glossies. Swamped with requests, the casting department managed to trim the hungering hordes to some 5,000 interviews. Of those, just over 100 finalists were given screen tests at $300 a shot. The entire stunt had ballooned beyond belief, and still not a single worthy actor had emerged.

By now, Harry Cohn was squirming on the end of his own carefully baited hook. Something very near panic was beginning to set in. Director Mamoulian, the while, was trying to maintain some semblance of business as usual and

GOLDEN BOY (1939). With Lee J. Cobb and Don Beddoe

GOLDEN BOY (1939). With Barbara Stanwyck

took to casting the supporting roles. The part of Joe Bonaparte's sister, Anna, had itself come to be a minor headache and, with Columbia's resources exhausted, Paramount was asked to send over screen tests of young actresses. Mamoulian and his producer, William Perlberg, were wading midway through the batch when the test of Rebecca Wasson was screened. Something jolted the bleary-eyed Perlberg, but it wasn't Wasson. A second runthrough told it all—that agreeable school-boy, Holden, fumbling his way through the scene with her, was the very raw material they had been seeking for *Golden Boy*. Mamoulian later recalled, "He was essentially himself. He had freshness, charm, a certain attractive sincerity. He had a relaxed quality that made for naturalness. All those things were more important than acting finesse. With those other things, he could be made to act." At least, that was the proposition.

The wheels began to turn furiously. Cohn was shown the test and reacted with something less than hosannas. A second test was arranged while a deal was worked out with Paramount to purchase half of the $50-a-week contract in the event Holden was signed for the picture. The second test did little more to sway Cohn, but by then he was willing to defer to his producer and director, if only to get himself off the spot. Within twenty-four hours, Holden was signed.

From her safe vantage in Pasadena, Mary Beedle had long believed that movie casts consisted of scantily clothed chorus girls paddling underwater. Skeptical as she was, when Bill returned home one evening with news of his good fortune, neither she nor her husband wished to discourage him. The die was cast, sanctioned, and celebrated. The following morning, April 8, witnessed the start of a painstaking metamorphosis.

As originally written by Clifford Odets and staged by Harold Clurman, Joe Bonaparte was an improbable but pleasingly puzzling character, a victim of conflicting talents that could neither meld nor be denied. An Italian tough off the streets, Joe has grown up feisty and able to use his hands. As fate would have it, he is equally able to use his hands on the violin, with a touch bordering on virtuosity. A corps of meddlers and parasites attempts to tell Joe what he wants, when all Joe really wants is happiness, a share of fame, and to be left alone. Succumbing at last to the temptation of flash success, he becomes a contending boxer, but fights with too little conviction and too much conscience. In the end, the very impulses for which Joe craves resolution speed him to a tragic death.

It was an exacting part, made all the more so on film. Where Luther Adler capitalized on the broadness of gesture and the masking of make-up afforded the proscenium player, Holden faced the probing realism of the screen. And, where Clurman dodged the explicit demands of Bonaparte's musicianship and ringsmanship by blocking both offstage, Mamoulian knew that movie audiences would not tolerate evasion. Joe Bonaparte had to be shaped from the ground up.

For Holden, the molding started immediately and ran like a high-speed assembly line. He reported to the studio each morning at 7:30 for what was modestly termed "make-up." It was more like a daily session with Dr. Frankenstein, running the gamut from hair dyeing, brilliantining, and curling, through facial and body make-up, all the way to periodic thinning of chest hair. Whatever the price in pride, Mrs. Beedle's little boy always managed to appear on the set by 8:30, looking convincingly Italian.

GOLDEN BOY (1939). With Barbara Stanwyck and Adolphe Menjou

In the harried half-hour before shooting, Bill rehearsed the day's lines with his private dialogue coach, Hugh MacMullan, and, time permitting, would then ethnicize his enunciation with the help of Mario, a local restauranteur hired for expert advice on inflection and hand gesture.

Shooting continued until six, sometimes with, sometimes without a break for lunch. From there, it was to the music department for lessons in violin fingering with Columbia's music director Morris Stoloff, a quick thirty minutes for dinner, a brief nap, and then over to the gymnasium for boxing lessons with "Newsboy" Brown. Home by ten, Bill would begin to memorize the next day's lines with MacMullan, whom Mamoulian, never one to squander time, had installed as a roommate in Bill's flat.

The pace never slackened, and the inevitable traces of stress began to show on the novice. He became irritable, alternately shy and bossy, even offering advice to Mamoulian in a number of instances. If Bill seemed out of his depth, it was only because he had been plunged headlong into deep water and told to swim. He took to phoning his mother five and six times a day, just to talk. Mamoulian took to phoning Harry Cohn, just to see if some colossal error in judgment hadn't been made.

Two weeks into the shooting, Bill Holden did what any normal, twenty-one-year-old would have done under the circumstances—he suffered a nervous collapse. There was a great deal of nail-biting as Bill missed shooting for the next two days, and Columbia's own Golden Boy seemed a sure bet to tarnish. For all the vast theatrical experience represented in the production, no one could quite figure how to siphon Bill's talent without draining Bill. No one, that is, except Barbara Stanwyck.

Taking matters into her own capable hands, she began to work with Bill instead of on him. She encouraged him to understand his dialogue, and to that end, personally rehearsed with him after hours, tirelessly taking pains to set the subtle moods and tones upon which a performance can pivot. She sought to minimize other distractions by requesting a halt to publicity interviews and a closed set. Miss Stanwyck even extended her charity to the shooting itself, permitting many shared scenes to be printed according to Bill's performance instead of her own.

The other cast members took the cue, shaming so chronic a scene thief as Adolphe Menjou into less grabbing and more giving. A rare spirit of cooperation settled in just long enough for Bill to regain his footing. With the continued coaching of Stanwyck and the recent wisdom of his own trials, he was at last getting inside a breathing character.

The cozy lull passed and shooting returned to its exhausting tempo, only now Holden kept stride emotionally and professionally. As an early safeguard, Harry Cohn had tacked an additional three weeks onto the shooting schedule. *Golden Boy* was wrapped up a full three days before the original deadline.

If it can be said that Hollywood tilled a bumper crop of classic movies in a single year, then that year would have to be 1939. With offerings as diverse as *Gone With the Wind, Mr. Smith Goes to Washington, The Wizard of Oz,* and *Stagecoach, Golden Boy* made little more than a ripple where it might have made a splash in an average season.

Granted, the film has its faults. Mamoulian's transcription goes far toward enlarging the play, but there are still awkward vestiges of staginess. As Joe's boxing manager, Menjou is his usual flap-tongued self, playing to the balcony. No less distracting is Lee J. Cobb's mannered rendition of

GOLDEN BOY (1939). With Barbara Stanwyck

the culture-hungry Mr. Bonaparte, but, forgivably, this was his first screen role after years on the stage, and if he sports an accent that might be used to top a pizza, he nevertheless records many touching moments. The supporting roles are, for the most part, trimly executed by Edward Brophy, Sam Levene, and Joseph Calleia, who, perhaps, brings a touch of caricature to his gangster promoter (played on stage by Elia Kazan).

Golden Boy's real muscle is its non-theatricality. Much of the dialogue is moved outdoors, softening the less wieldy lines. And Mamoulian's unflinchingly graphic attention to Joe's music and boxing gives the story a credible lift. Nor is any of the directorial punch wasted on Holden. His early off-screen anxiety feeds magically into Joe Bonaparte's own explosive temperament, and his surging confidence neatly parallels Joe's ascent. The meticulous care given the more technical aspects of the role pays off in spades, with Bill proficient as violinist and pugilist. At the same time, his range of dramatic expression registers honestly over the difficult emotional terrain of Bonaparte's stormy personality. The final two reels, which belong almost exclusively to Holden and demand one wrenching passage after another, are eloquent testimony to his motion picture matriculation.

Admittedly, Barbara Stanwyck, whose noble tramp Lorna Moon is torn between loyalty to Menjou and love of Holden, is the picture's titan. She inspires fine ensemble playing and serves as a willing springboard for Holden's more demanding moments. Certainly, the most powerful scenes are those between Stanwyck and her pupil.

Considering the gamble, *Golden Boy* did very sound business at the box office and won its share of good notices when it opened that September. Beyond scattered niggling grievances, few critics disliked Holden's performance. Most marveled at this bold debut and gladly trumpeted the news that a new star had been delivered. What bothered the critics most was that Joe and Lorna had been permitted to fade out in a warm embrace, instead of the shattering auto wreck of the Odets original. But the actors could hardly be blamed for Hollywood's obsession with happy endings.

Of his new star, director Mamoulian had some discerning comments. "On the screen, you will see an uncanny thing. 'Golden Boy' actually grows, matures, under your very eyes. It is easy to grow old, with a change of make-up, a change of posture, a change of voice. It is more difficult to mature. Unless that happens inside, nothing

shows. No star could have put this across as Bill does."

But Bill was all humility. He knew the value of Barbara Stanwyck's tutoring, but rather than waste words on her to the press, he said it with flowers, two dozen roses worth, and has done so every year since, on the film's anniversary.

Bill Beedle had braved the racking rites of passage and emerged William Holden, "star." And yet the glitter and fame seemed hollow to him. "I don't think anybody had as much determination and ambition as I had the day I started making this movie. Then, one day, I went to the opening of *Golden Boy* and saw my name up on the marquee. There was my name in lights, and I suddenly knew that it didn't mean a damn thing to me." William Holden was ready to become an actor.

"I'm in pictures for the duration of the public's interest. I love the work."
— to *Photoplay,* July, 1940

A STAR IS BORED

In Hollywood, there is such a thing as becoming too famous too fast. Fearful that their ward could prove to be a one-shot wonder, Columbia eagerly loaned out Holden to let him continue cutting his actor's teeth at another studio's expense. They might just as well have slapped a postage stamp on his forehead—his next three films were made at three different studios.

Holden first journeyed to Warner Brothers for *Invisible Stripes,* another of the prison yarns by former Sing Sing Warden Lewis E. Lawes. By 1940, this cycle of the genre was beginning to yellow at the edges, but Lloyd Bacon supplied brisk direction and managed to pump life into the story of two parolees. As the once burned, twice cautious ex-con, George Raft leaves a bland impression of the pitfalls to rehabilitation. Humphrey Bogart is much more flavorful as his hardened prison pal who knows better than to retire from the rackets.

Holden is left with the stock role of Raft's grease-monkey kid brother, who, with some simple arithmetic, notices that the wages of sin far outdraw those of a mechanic. It falls to big brother to try to keep the kid's nose clean while walking his own straight and narrow. Failing that, Raft secretly turns to crime, delivering the boodle to his family under the flimsy guise of tractor sales commissions. The upshot of it all is that Raft and Bogart end up stopping a few dozen bullets, while Holden ends up starting his own garage and wrecker service with their loot.

Considering its ready-made nature, the film culled positive reviews, especially from the Communist *Daily Worker* whose critic applauded a scene in which Raft angrily refuses work as a labor spy. Bogart turns in an engaging performance in transition from his snivelling thirties villainy to his cynical forties valor, but Holden's performance is strangely unsettling. He seems to be plumbing the role for more than is there, and, rather than overact, appears restive. In many ways, his acting is too intense to blend with the highly stylized pulp of the Warners' milieu.

If Holden was after a plum role, he found it at his next home away from home, United Artists, which wanted him for the upcoming filming of Thornton Wilder's Pulitzer Prize-winning play, *Our Town*

INVISIBLE STRIPES (1940). With George Raft

(1940). Instead of a showy veneer of class, producer Sol Lesser committed himself to a film that would enrich the work without disturbing its integrity. To his credit, this marriage of theater and film meshes splendidly as an ideal version of Wilder's philosophical fable about the eternal verities of life and death in an American town.

William Cameron Menzies' production design strikes a delicate balance between the bare stage of the original play and a fullblown studio replication, filling an atmosphere that is properly setbound, though not stagey. Aaron Copeland contributes a score which is both discreetly supportive and distinctly its own, and Sam Wood directs with restraint, orchestrating the potentially clashing elements into a filmed theatrical event.

Frank Craven was wisely asked to repeat his stage role as the wry Narrator who weaves in and out of the story, as was Martha Scott with the role of Emily Webb. The remaining roles fell to such veteran character actors as Thomas Mitchell, Guy Kibbee, Fay Bainter, and Beulah Bondi. Holden was given the meaty role of George Gibbs, son of the town doctor (Mitchell); a good-hearted, if occasionally vain and dull-witted, all-American boy. To that apple-pie extent, Holden might have seemed a natural for the part, but he, emphatically, was not typecast.

This time, Holden refused to shrink in any way from the role or shooting routine. Scrubbed and steady, he presents George Gibbs as something of an amiable dunderhead. His acting is even but textured, and a snug control is apparent, underscored in scenes with Martha Scott (George's neighbor, then sweetheart and spouse) who, in her first screen work, tends to overproject.

All told, *Our Town* is a masterpiece both as a document of filmed theater and as film. Like the play before it, the screenplay by Thornton Wilder, Frank Craven, and Harry Chandlee guards the simple sanctity of the characters and does not trade in stereotypes. Its only compromise is in permitting Emily to live through childbirth rather than die as in the original ending—an unnecessary hedging since death is not downbeat within the play's context of the cyclic flow of nature. At any rate, the screenplay does retain Emily's death vision and refrains from any further tinkering.

With three major films to his credit, Holden finally went to work for the studio that hired him. Paramount placed him in a collegiate comedy called *Those Were the Days* (1940), based on the *Good Ole Siwash* stories by George Fitch, and celebrated the event by

OUR TOWN (1940). The wedding of George and Emily (Martha Scott)

billing the young star's name over the title.

The plot, a nostalgic glance at the high-spirited mindlessness of college in 1904, has all the weight of meringue. Despite the energized efforts of Bonita Granville, Ezra Stone, and Judith Barrett, the film slogs along out of proportion to its short running time. Even Holden's bouncy Petey Simmons (a conceited, rascally freshman) cannot rescue this from a doily-like quaintness. Frankly, there is little to be done with episodes that run like a hand-cranked nickelodeon. Aside from a brief, salty turn by William Frawley as a jailbird, *Those Were the Days* is an eminently forgettable motion picture.

William Holden was sorely in need of a shift from frolicsome fare and Columbia had just the thing, a Western. What with the surprising success of John Ford's *Stagecoach* two years earlier, the horse opera was now legitimate, and Harry Cohn was ready to cash in on the trend with a film called *Arizona* (1941). True to the setting, the lead came to Holden on a ricochet. Director Wesley Ruggles had wanted Gary Cooper for the role of California-bound Peter Muncie, but Cooper was tied up with Sam Goldwyn at the time. Joel McCrea was then announced for the part until more complications set in and Holden was drafted at one-tenth the salary.

Shooting on location in Arizona,

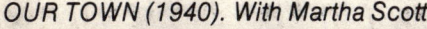

OUR TOWN (1940). With Martha Scott

THOSE WERE THE DAYS (1940). With Bonita Granville

Ruggles ran up astronomical costs on what amounts to a laundry list Western of good guys, bad guys, Indians, stampedes, and the ever punctual cavalry. Suffice it to say that Holden plays the guy in the white hat, variously strumming and gunning his way into the heart of the heroine, Jean Arthur. Through it all, he acquits himself nicely on horseback, and never blanches before Miss Arthur's dynamic work.

Had the movie not bogged down in historical asides and meandering subplots, *Arizona* might have been more than an expensive mistake. That, and the foolishly flagrant age disparity between Arthur and Holden, reduced the outing to something of a labored exercise, showing Columbia that their initial $25-a-week star was versatile and thriving.

The Holden character repertoire stretched again with *I Wanted Wings* (1941), a modest service picture, passable only when it stops straining to resuscitate the hoary tradition of the femme fatale. The plot hinges on the exploits of an unlikely trio of cadets winning their wings en route to a commission in the Army Air Corps. Suppressing a suspect British accent, Ray Milland plays a Long Island playboy, accustomed to the gilt-edged life. Wayne Morris supplies the familiar role of a former college football hero, a thoroughly likable

ARIZONA (1940). With Jean Arthur

I WANTED WINGS (1941). With Ray Milland and Wayne Morris

schlemiel. Holden rounds out the threesome as a just-plain-folks garage mechanic trying to better himself and forget a mysterious woman from his past.

As it happens, that woman is the anything-but-mysterious novice nymphet, Veronica Lake, shuffling through her first starring role. And it is the tangle of romantic detours inserted for her and Constance Moore that soddenly keeps *Wings* from ever getting off the ground. The initially trim aviation-initiation drama turns into 131 minutes of eye-strain.

Mitchell Leisen, brought in to direct after a false start precipitated by the skittish Miss Lake, helps salvage the film from utter bafflement. His close work with aerial photographer, Elmer Dyer, produces some of the most fluid and captivating moments. The location footage from Randolph and Kelly Fields helps the cause, but cannot of its own overcome the generally tepid acting. Milland serves up a warmed-over version of Cary Grant, while Miss Lake, whose visible talent seems only to come together in plunging necklines, masquerades as a miniature Marlene Dietrich, more tramp than vamp.

The casting of Morris and Holden is of special interest since Morris had, at one time, been a front-runner in the *Golden Boy* sweepstakes. His burly gridiron

TEXAS (1941). With Glenn Ford

bonehead is passable, though unimaginative. Holden, on the other hand, delivers a complex portrait of a self-doubting, often-manipulated mechanic who overcomes a volatile defeatism, only to be thwarted by Miss Lake's flimsy floozy. With Brian Donlevy performing blandly as the cadet's flight instructor, Holden easily walked off with the best notices. Given the timeliness of a film nominally about military preparedness with America on the brink of war, *I Wanted Wings* rode in atop a patriotic groundswell.

Not one to burn his britches behind him, Holden teamed with Glenn Ford for another round of sagebrush in George Marshall's *Texas* (1941). Unlike the costly and plodding *Arizona,* this movie sweeps along with much of the zip and humor that Marshall had injected earlier into his *Destry Rides Again* (1939). Here, the flinty Edgar Buchanan is on hand as is the durable Claire Trevor to lend support to the young stars.

The standard story concerns two former Civil War confreres who, as civilians, find themselves on opposite sides of the law, one a drover, the other a rustler. As the pal gone afoul of the law, Holden furnishes an unfussy character whose final gesture of gallantry is quite credible. *Texas* gallops along at a steady clip up to an ending that leaves Holden biting the dust and Ford filling Miss Trevor's open arms.

The movie worked a chemistry that proved magnetic at the box office. There was even a footnote to its charmed existence when it was found that the longhorn steers purchased for the occasion had fattened in the course of shooting, bringing a handsome profit when resold. The steers weren't the only ones getting fat off the Western. Whatever else the industry thought of them, unassuming genre pieces like *Texas* were often bankrolling the award-winning prestige pictures.

There were many who envied Bill Holden the reputed lot of the young movie star: fame, fortune, and fornication. The truth, however, was that, though his star was on the rise, it was by no means fixed in the Hollywood galaxy, and financially, he was grossing the relatively paltry sum of $150 per week. As for the alleged amour, it need only be said that he was still essentially the God-fearing kid from O'Fallon. Security in cash and celebrity would be years in the offing, but the anemic love-life was soon to be remedied.

Knowing Bill's bashfulness, roommate Hugh MacMullan volunteered as resident cupid. While Bill was at Warners for *Invisible Stripes,* MacMullan introduced him to a close friend and fellow New York emigre, Brenda

With wife Ardis (Brenda Marshall) in 1942

THE REMARKABLE ANDREW (1942). With Brian Donlevy

Marshall, a Warners contract player who had appeared opposite Errol Flynn in *The Sea Hawk* and was on steady assignment to programmers and an occasional "A" film. Instead of the headline-hungry starlet he half expected, Bill was greeted by an elegantly personable brunette, witty, sensible, and refined. Their first date was in September of 1940 and soon they were constant companions. But a dash to the altar simply was not in the cards. Besides their respective career obligations, Brenda (actually named Ardis) was tussling through divorce proceedings involving some sensitive litigation over custody of her daughter, Virginia. Bill remained a patient suitor, certain he had found the woman of his dreams.

Ardis' marriage to actor Richard Huston Gaines had curdled long ago in New York, and Holden's devotion meant a great deal to her. Her divorce was finalized in the early summer of 1941, and, at the first opportunity, she and Bill were wed in Las Vegas, a full twenty-one months after they had first met. The courtship was longer than most Hollywood marriages.

But their wedding ceremony was anything but auspicious. A Congregationalist Church service had been arranged, and Bill, in Los Angeles for some shooting, was to fly in that evening with his best man, Brian Donlevy. What with set delays and bad weather, it was 3:00 A.M. before the weary groom arrived, and the minister had long since turned in for the night. It was 4:00 Sunday morning before another preacher could be collared. The knot was tied and toasted with a champagne breakfast, which left Bill just enough time to hop a plane back to Los Angeles to continue shooting. No sooner was his work completed than Ardis was called away to Canada for some location footage of her own, and after a chain of mishaps that included the newlyweds' undergoing successive emergency appendectomies, it was three months before they finally shared a week of breakfasts as man and wife. Obviously, something had to be done. By mutual consent, Ardis retired from acting, even though her current weekly income of $750 was five times that of Bill's. The Holdens settled into their new ranch home in the Toluca Lake section of the San Fernando Valley.

By 1942, Holden had been put through the assorted paces of studio casting and had compiled a respectable track record. Paramount was now ready to experiment with him in comedy, and turned Bill loose on Dalton Trumbo's *The Remarkable Andrew*.

The project had first been seeded by Trumbo's idea of invoking the ghosts of America's founding fathers to guide a contemporary idealist through a personal political dilemma. Paramount saluted the concept and urged Trumbo to present it first as a popular novel before going to script. He obliged, spinning a fable about a small town city clerk, Andrew Long, who stumbles upon evidence of corruption within the local officialdom. Long, a paragon of wide-eyed righteousness and an unflagging admirer of Andrew Jackson, wrestles with his conscience before choosing to divulge his findings, whereupon he is bounced out of office by the wily grafters. As a debt to Long's grandfather (who had saved his life at the Battle of New Orleans), the ghost of Andrew Jackson visits young Andrew in his hour of need. In due course, Old Hickory, something of a blustery sot, sees the clerk through the crisis, but not before summoning the spirits of George Washington, Ben Franklin, Thomas Jefferson, John Marshall, Jesse James, and some obscure Regular of the Continental Army, for counsel.

For all of its star-spangled whimsy, the novel sold remarkably well, and Paramount stood ready to complete the bargain. Holden was cast as Long, and his best man, Brian Donlevy, was asked to play Jackson. With Ellen Drew added as Long's long-suffering fiancée, the film began shooting on location in Colorado. It soon became clear that Holden was the perfect choice for this Frank Capra-esque dogged democrat. (After all, Holden's mother, née Mary Bell, was a collateral descendent of George Washington.) What's more, he was sufficiently resourceful as a comic actor to avoid the yawning pitfalls of fatuousness that surround such fancy. Holden matches Donlevy's hammy Jackson with a pop-eyed, hand-wringing Long. His balminess dovetails nicely into the sober-sided city clerk who delivers the penultimate lecture on the fascistic menace posed to democracy by chummy municipal ne'er-do-wells. In what was, at best, a mixed blessing, the press almost unanimously liked Holden better than the movie, which they found frivolous in wartime.

After giving so handy a performance, Holden deserved better than he was about to get in his next pair of movies, *The Fleet's In* and *Meet The Stewarts* (both 1942). Just the same, he was plugged into these potboilers and told to "smile."

A second Paramount refitting of the bawdy 1935 stage musical *Sailor Beware, The Fleet's In* foundered from the outset. No one had paused to wonder whether Holden could sing, and it was soon discovered that the former choir boy had a consistent voice, that is, consistently one fifth below the

THE REMARKABLE ANDREW (1942). With Harlan Briggs and Ellen Drew

THE FLEET'S IN (1942). With Dorothy Lamour

melody. So he didn't sing. But in light of the impoverished material and the scantily adequate performing of Dorothy Lamour, Eddie Bracken, and Betty Hutton, it would have made little difference if Holden had the larynx of Caruso. The movie is a hodgepodge of specialty acts that bears harsh testimony to the fact that, by 1942, Paramount still didn't know how to make a musical.

Columbia was no more discreet in its use of Holden in *Meet The Stewarts*. Based on Elizabeth Dunn's magazine stories of Candy and Mike Stewart, this is a comedy that never quite comes off the page. It has, as its trite premise, the marriage of the lordly (she) and the lowly (he) and the attendant problems of trying to corset expensive tastes and habits (hers) into a petite budget (his).

The situations tick off like clockwork in the manner of forties antiseptic marital comedies that reached their final, banal bloom in the television situation comedies of the fifties. *Meet The Stewarts* inspired reactions like "innocuous" and "ingratiating"—every bit as indelible as skywritung. Through it all, Holden bravely pasted on his best grin, but it seemed to be wearing perilously thin.

Bill Holden's next screen appearance was to be his last before Army enlistment. *Young and Willing* was actually shot in 1942 by

MEET THE STEWARTS (1942). With Frances Dee

Paramount, but was sold to United Artists and held for release until the fall of 1943. While it is a peppy rendition of a successful Francis Swann play called *Out of the Frying Pan,* it was not especially worth waiting for, churning an effervescence that nearly sours into dyspepsia.

The story has to do with an odd assortment of aspiring thespians living dormitory style in a Greenwich Village brownstone. As might be expected, there is virtually no income and the expenses are blithely attended by a flighty rich girl. There are a number of twists involving a pesky cousin, a pregnancy, and an eccentric neighbor who turns out to be a top theatrical producer, but in the end, it all becomes haphazard.

Gnarls aside, the plot still does what it is supposed to do—provide acting calisthenics for a number of young contract players. Garble-voiced Eddie Bracken is present, diligently chewing the scenery, with Barbara Britton constantly swooning, Martha O'Driscoll simpering, and Florence MacMichael grating as a bubble-headed, Betty Boop-voiced snitch. With no lift from a plainly disinterested Robert Benchley, the burden of saving matters from amateurish drudgery falls to Holden and a shapely young Susan Hayward. They are more than equal to the call.

The ravishing Miss Hayward im-

YOUNG AND WILLING (1943). With Eddie Bracken, Barbara Britton, Susan Hayward, and Martha O'Driscoll

parts an assured grace and style, and Holden serves as the movie's comic metronome with a gait and timing that is often absent in Edward Griffith's direction. Holden's kinetic performance almost—but not quite—cloaks the fact that he abhorred such lightweight material.

When, in 1942, Bill Holden enlisted in the Army Air Corps on his twenty-fourth birthday, he did so with a curious sense of relief. Of his dozen films to date, he believed he could only look to one or two with any sense of accomplishment or pride. Even at this early phase, he felt his progress as a screen actor sputtering for want of challenging roles. In the face of dwindling prospects, the service may not have held any answers, but it certainly offered a refuge from the increasingly frustrating swirl of Hollywood life.

"I was always that damned boy next door. I went to college in Those Were the Days, *grew up in* Our Town, *was an air cadet in* I Wanted Wings. *The name of my character was 'Smilin' Jim.' I hated his guts."*

— to *McCall's,* July, 1962

THE WAR ENDS, THE BATTLE BEGINS

William Holden never saw combat duty. Like most other entertainers turned soldier, he was kept stateside and held to public relations.

Nevertheless, he had signed up a scant eight months after marriage — the first Hollywood family man to enlist. He left behind a barely rooted home life, a wife who was one month pregnant, and a career that was beginning to wobble. These, and other events were to hurl him into the most turbulent period of his young life.

It all started innocently enough. Refusing the special privileges often accorded celebrities, Holden entered the Army Air Corps Officers Candidate School in Miami Beach, Florida as a private, legally changing his name from Beedle upon entry. He completed the program, received his commission as a second lieutenant, and was promptly assigned to entertainment duty in Texas. In the late fall of 1943, Holden managed to secure leave to be with Ardis, then within days of childbirth. He arrived home on November 16 and the next day became the father of a baby boy, Peter Westfield Holden, named in part for Bill's younger brother, Bob Westfield Beedle. The leave expired and Bill was forced to abandon Ardis to the toils of maternity, but not before the proud parents wrote to brother Bob, a pilot in the South Pacific, telling him of his new nephew namesake. Bob returned a letter, glowing over the news—it was the last the family would hear from him. His Hellcat fighter was brought down by enemy fire off the coast of New Britain.

It's impossible to gauge the death's impact upon Holden. At the very least, it brought him closer to an understanding of his own mortality and jolted other outlooks into perspective. One thing was certain, William Holden began to assume a life view that was worlds apart from his pre-service days.

The next phase of Holden's tour of duty was divided between Texas and Connecticut, with a portion of that time spent in a walk-on for an Office of War Information

BLAZE OF NOON (1947). With William Bendix, Anne Baxter, and Sonny Tufts

recruiting two-reeler, which Clark Gable was putting together for the Defense Department. Entitled *Wings Up* (1943), it clumsily attempts to dramatize the need for capable aviation officers. Among the Hollywood personalities pictured are Gilbert Roland and Robert Preston, and a fleeting glimpse of Holden receiving his wings with a beaming Ardis at his side. The film had very little to recommend it, even by recruiting standards, and went unused.

For the final nine months of service, Holden was reassigned to the Army's Motion Picture Unit in Culver City, putting him within easy reach of home. The fan magazines were quick to latch on to the story of Holden's ready enlistment, while bemoaning Ardis' lot as a war wife. Perhaps out of an embarrassment for such publicity, and an emotional sense of debt to his brother, Holden refused to pull strings for an early discharge, though it would have meant an important edge in the inevitable postwar rush to filmwork.

When Holden was mustered out of the service as a first lieutenant, in November of 1945, he faced $18,000 in back taxes, and a studio that was anxious to forget it had ever known him. If he harbored any illusions about executive sentiment and loyalty in Hollywood, they swiftly vanished. He later fumed about Paramount to *McCall's* Richard Gehman, "Do you know what that big benevolent company gave me while I was away? They gave me a Boy Scout knife and some soap samples. Oh boy, they really took care of their people." That would have seemed lavish in light of the treatment he was about to receive.

Holden no sooner started making the rounds at Paramount than he experienced the icy sting of the corporate cold shoulder. Studio executives, evidently gulled by their own fantasy work, were shaken to see that time did not stand still for their "boy next door." The face that greeted them was no longer the sincere, halting, visual equivalent of an American stammer; it was a man's face, slightly fleshy, somewhat lined, with the features deepened. It was a maturely comely face, to be sure, but Paramount was not convinced it had a place in its gallery of stars.

Stalled by the studio—mention was made only of a role in the filming of the popular wartime comedy, *Dear Ruth*—he was suddenly struck by the fact that acting had ceased to be some adolescent flirtation. It wasn't just something he did well, it was the only work he was trained to do. And it wasn't as if the studio was stringing along some starstruck snipe. He had a number of films to his credit, he had served his country well, and he was a husband and soon to be the father again (with the birth of another son, Scott). Deeply bitter, he was seeing the Hollywood factory for its salt.

In the hush of Holden's inactivity rumors began to fly. It was said that his last few pre-war films had been hampered by frequent tantrums, that he had become a troublemaker. The more vicious tongues insinuated that studio heads thought Holden lacking in the sex appeal necessary to hoist him from the ranks of juvenile. There was even one comment afoot in which an executive accused him of having a face that resembled "a baby's behind."

None of the prattle struck home, but neither did it do much for Holden's opinion of the press or the community. Something he could not shrug off, however, was his bleak financial condition. With Paramount dallying and dodging, there was talk of Ardis returning to work, just until a foothold could be regained. So she briefly became Brenda Marshall again, working opposite Alan Ladd in *Whispering Smith* (held for release until 1949). The incident wounded Holden's pride and possibly clouded his marriage for the first time. There was just no adjusting to the prospect of being a twenty-seven-year-old has-been.

BLAZE OF NOON (1947). With Anne Baxter

DEAR RUTH (1947). With Joan Caulfield and Billy De Wolfe

The Holdens were saved from any further jarring decisions when, eight months after his discharge, Bill received a call from Paramount. John Farrow would soon be directing a Frank Wead aviation drama about four brothers who leave carnival stunt-flying to help pioneer the first domestic air mail service. There was an opening for the romantic lead. Given a choice, Holden would not have selected this as a comeback vehicle, but under the circumstances he really didn't have much of a choice.

Blaze of Noon (1947) is an ordinary adventure movie that, with a firm directorial hand, might have been notable in the vein of Howard Hawks' *Only Angels Have Wings* (1939). It is a blank check setting, ripe for muscular acting and distinctive directing. Farrow, unfortunately, does not lend the requisite style, leaving the movie so slushy that it could be renamed *Blasé of Noon*.

The action revolves around the McDonald Brothers' aerial act which signs up to fly for the postal service in the barnstorming twenties. One by one, the brothers are killed or grounded, except for brother Colin (Holden), who happens also to be the only one with a wife and child. Prodded by some ambiguous mix of habit and male pride, Colin embarks on a perilous night flight and meets his maker. The film closes with the baptism of

Colin's child, as the minister intones, "He only half dies who leaves his image in his son", small reward for dad, who was last seen floating in the Hudson River.

Had there been an award for the most blond brawn in a feature length film, *Blaze of Noon* would have won, hands down. As the eldest McDonald, beefy Sonny Tufts looks a touch embalmed, which is excusable next to Sterling Hayden as number two son, who is every bit as limber as a ventriloquist's dummy. Holden, partly blonded for symmetry, comes up with the only truly layered performance, implying there is more to flying than suicidal idiocy.

Divided among veterans Howard da Sylva, William Bendix, and Anne Baxter (fresh from her Oscar winning role in *The Razor's Edge*), the supporting cast prevents the movie from growing untidy. The other chief attraction is Paul Mantz' dazzling aerial stunt-work, with Holden too often lost in the shuffle.

Lest it ever be said that Paramount was untrue to its word, Holden was at long last deposited in the often-mentioned *Dear Ruth* (1947). The Arthur Sheekman screenplay of the Norman Krasna play boiled down to little more than a glorified blind date, brought about by the precocious firebrand younger daughter of a Kew Gardens judge. It seems she has maintained a faithful and intimate correspondence with a bombardier serving in Europe, while posing and signing as her older sister, Ruth. Inevitably, the smitten young serviceman appears unannounced on short leave, hoping to meet and marry the mysterious pen pal. Rather than expose the truth, which would be dastardly and unpatriotic to boot, the family begins a diversionary charade, complicated a trifle by the fact that the real Ruth is already engaged to be married. The story unwinds as expected, with the suitor eventually discovering the truth, by which time Ruth has genuinely fallen for him in a finale where the two wed hastily and flee, all under the nose of the unsuspecting fiancé.

The foolery might have been overdrawn for what was really a rather tame middle-class comedy, had not the wit justified the means. Luckily, the sharpness of the dialogue plows through the thicket. In a respite from his many tyrannical roles, Edward Arnold is grumpily affectionate as the enduring father, and Mary Philips wryly placid as his endearing wife. Mona Freeman is irritating to order as the brattish younger daughter, and the eternal snit, Billy De Wolfe, is the jilted fiancé. Quirkily, though, the two key roles, those of Ruth and Lt. Seacroft, are

VARIETY GIRL (1947). With Ray Milland

parched in their conception, giving Joan Caulfield and Holden precious little with which to work. Holden's role is unflattering in the extreme, requiring merely a mindless momentum and a regular flashing of the dental work.

In spite of a cluttered mounting, *Dear Ruth* delivered its laughs and found a large audience. Holden may not have sparkled, but his fortunes rose several notches with the picture. His real coup was offscreen. Noticing that the wardrobe department had been budgeted $650 to secure a lieutenant's uniform for him, Holden shrewdly sold them his own ready-to-wear government issue for a bargain $500, still netting a neat profit. It had taken some time, but he was getting wise to the Hollywood hustle.

One of the movie genres of the forties was the "all-star" musical in which the studio brought together its contract players in a revue-like format which would have them singing and dancing, performing in comedy sketches, or simply making an appearance. Paramount's wartime contribution had been *Star-Spangled Rhythm* (1942), and in 1947, the studio slapped together another creaky showcase for its players in *Variety Girl,* ostensibly dedicated to the Variety Clubs of America.

The movie's thin strand of story centers on a pair of starstruck young women who, through some inadvertent name swapping, cut a wide swathe across the soundstages and backlots of Paramount. The passive Mary Hatcher and the pushy Olga San Juan lunge about, though hardly noticed for all the stardust. Among the stellar chattel seen are Barbara Stanwyck, Gary Cooper, Bing Crosby, Bob Hope, Alan Ladd, and Ray Milland, to name just a few, plus a healthy dose of lesser personalities, novelty acts, and directors.

With some inspection, William Holden can be spotted in the first reel, signing autographs outside Grauman's Theater. He quickly vanishes in the fray, not to reemerge until the final reel, warbling a single line in an interminable rendition of "Harmony." One of the better digressions from the limping plot is a musical interlude delivered with savage savvy by Spike Jones and his City Slickers.

After the annoying anonymity of such second-hand vaudeville, Holden went to RKO and *Rachel and the Stranger* (1948), a sober sleeper of a movie which was the first truly bright spot in his postwar work. Never grasping for glamour or false luster, this account of frontier life even resists a tempting homespun folksiness, contenting itself with a subdued, calico-like

RACHEL AND THE STRANGER (1948). With Loretta Young

APARTMENT FOR PEGGY (1948). With Jeanne Crain

narrative fabric.

Holden provides an expertly rustic tailoring of the halting, stern homesteader, mourning the sudden death of his treasured wife. Fretful that his son will turn "woodsy" without a woman's civilizing hand, he resorts to a second marriage, for practical purposes alone. Looking authentic but fetching in drab garb, Loretta Young plays the hapless bondswoman who becomes his bride and housekeeper. Life for her turns to tedium until the seasonal visit of a trapper-huntsman (drawled and swaggered by Robert Mitchum) who takes an interest in her that is something more than neighborly. The temperate homesteader, Holden, puzzles over the smooth flirtation before conceding "Sometimes I think I don't rightly understand people." More pithy insights follow fast on the heels of an Indian raid, which settles matters for all, with Holden and Young warmly embracing and Mitchum back to his wandering ways.

Snug direction by ex-actor Norman Foster (late of Charlie Chan and Mr. Moto movies) and dialogue by Waldo Salt captures a certain tonal truth without sacrificing humor or drive. Fortified by the unfrilly acting, *Rachel and the Stranger* is a model of cinematic simplicity. Any chance of box-office obscurity was averted by Mitchum's pre-release sensationalized arrest for possession of marijuana. The scandalized public turned out to see what film this degenerate had made, and was treated to a simon-pure slice of Americana.

However harnessed by prior casting, Holden had taken a stubborn stride forward. It was time for another step backward and, on loan-out, Fox had just the thing in *Apartment for Peggy* (1948). A cozy, moralizing comedy of doubtful good sense, it was written and directed by George Seaton, who had registered a startling success the year before with his *Miracle on 34th Street*. Repeating in an eccentric, if less fanciful role, is Edmund Gwenn, whose Kris Kringle had won him a supporting Oscar for *Miracle*. Here, Gwenn is a pompous philosophy professor who gathers that suicide is preferable to facing his dotage without his recently deceased wife.

A fluttery, impetuous, and downright impossible Peggy (Jeanne Crain) yanks the tweedy academician away from self-pity when she heckles him into renting the attic of his house to herself and her husband. Holden is the defeatist spouse, Jason, who, though resuming chemistry studies (sic) under the GI bill, is forever on the verge of deserting college for a go at a fast buck. Miss Crain has her hands full keeping Holden in school, Gwenn out of the grave, and a watchful eye on her own pregnancy. When it seems that something has to give, everything gives, with Holden flitting off to Chicago to peddle used cars, Gwenn again keen on suicide, and the baby miscarrying. The scene is now set for the final rectitude, resplendent with sermonizing. Holden returns for an eleventh-hour bid at exams, and just for an encore, finds time to scold the suicide-bent Gwenn, using some soldierly leverage, "I can think of an awful lot of fellas that would've liked to have had the choice that you have now." With this oratorical flourish, Gwenn is shamed into living, as all are restored to former status, including Miss Crain's Peggy, who, underneath the cheery dizziness, seems to annoy everyone, including Miss Crain.

Holding ground against Gwenn's cutesy mugging and Crain's heartstring tugging, Holden was fortunate to get out of this one alive. He played Jason explosively, but it was difficult to determine whether it was the character or the actor who had the short fuse.

Rudolph Maté may well have noted this volcanic trait because he soon convinced Holden to take the role of the skittish psychopath in *The Dark Past* (1948), a remake of *Blind Alley*, Columbia's 1939 thriller with Chester Morris and

Ralph Bellamy. Under Maté's taut direction, the shadow-bathed, crisply acted second production is a mainstream piece of forties *film noir*. Replete with close-cropped coiffure and a terse handling of the-average-man-gone-mad, Holden is wonderfully suited to the genre.

Al Walker is a notorious prison escapee who, with his gang, commandeers the vacation house of psychiatrist Andrew Collins. Before one can say "Oedipus Rex," Collins ferrets and traces the criminal's blood lust to a recurring nightmare which unlocks a childhood trauma involving mother love and conspiratorial fratricide. This supersonic psychoanalysis so unburdens Walker of his trigger-happy hatred that he is unable to do battle when the police arrive, and he is escorted off without a whimper.

Simplistic and dollar-book Freud as it is, *The Dark Past* introduced Holden to a style of character complexity to which he was best attuned. His Walker is savage, but also pathetically winsome, an introverted man whose tangled mental workings lie just below the sur-

THE DARK PAST (1948). With Nina Foch

THE MAN FROM COLORADO (1949). With Edgar Buchanan and Ellen Drew

face. Lee J. Cobb fills the marginally pedantic role of the psychiatrist with a minimum of the histrionics he had used opposite Holden in *Golden Boy,* nine years earlier. Together, Cobb and Holden scale the rocky mindscape of this psychodrama that was branded by many as a bleeding-heart slant on crime. Such attitudinizing was definitely beyond the movie's scope. Commenting for *The New York Times,* A.H. Weiler had the truer line: "The mating of Freud and the films is not particularly new at this point," adding that *The Dark Past* was simply "one of the brighter results of that long association."

If anyone doubted that there could, in fact, be misplaced psychologizing in films, *The Man From Colorado* (1949) stood ready to settle the issue. Straining to cash in on trendy psychodramatics, this Western is counterfeit from the start. Glenn Ford and William Holden are once again Civil War buddies, reentering civilian life on the same side of the law, the former a judge, the latter his marshal. This time, it is Ford who suffers dementia, with a rather florid case of sadism (shooting first, asking questions later). Holden is driven outside of the law in order to see justice done, the very picture of a dashing, well-enameled outlaw. Following a glut of facile psychology and some horse operatics, the sadistic Ford meets an incendiary end, and the heroic Holden is restored to proper stature.

As the lean first half of a Western pair, *The Man From Colorado* actually whets the appetite for the non-psychotic, customarily clean carnage of *Streets of Laredo* (1949). Macdonald Carey, William Bendix, and Holden are a scampish trio of highwaymen who become separated after a heist. Hoping to straddle the law for maximum gain, Bendix and Holden join the Texas Rangers, but are soon won over to righteous ways, and end up hunting their former partner, who meanwhile has sidled over to the nefarious side of lawlessness. There is an added pinch of plot thickening in the person of Mona Freeman, the object of affection for both Carey and Holden.

The action ravels and unravels according to form. Bendix hunts Carey. Carey guns Bendix. Holden stalks Carey. The flash-draw Carey wants a showdown. Miss Freeman intercedes with smoking rifle, erasing Carey and settling a few other questions as well. And nary a neurosis along the way.

The tired story and slapdash direction of Leslie Fenton is given a second wind by actors who bring personalized touches to their stock characters. Carey is something of

STREETS OF LAREDO (1949). As Jim Dawkins

an oily intellectual of a desperado, slinking about and teasing Miss Freeman in such extravagant language as "the antithesis of beauty and charm" in a departure from the traditional mustache twirling. Ever plump in the saddle, Bendix is fraternal and lovable, looking more like a fugitive bartender from the Bronx than a cowboy. Miss Freeman is troublesome and lovely, and Holden is always one step

MISS GRANT TAKES RICHMOND (1949). With James Gleason and Lucille Ball

ahead of the scenery, amiable and physical, doing his own stuntwork and looking the part, which is about all the authenticity one could ask for.

Battling narrative lapses, obvious process-shot insertions within Technicolor location footage, inept framing, and even discontinuity of lighting within a single scene, the cast performs handily down the line.

No one had to tell the by now much-Westerned Holden that there was more to acting and timing than dismounting a horse on cue. The most severe test of timing is in comic acting, and the most severe test of comic acting is having to appear with a practiced comedian, or, as is the case in *Miss Grant Takes Richmond* (1949), comedienne. Stiffening his upper lip, Holden co-starred with Lucille Ball in a Lloyd Bacon comedy about a brace of bookies driven to legitimacy by a bungling, bubbleheaded secretary. Holden had good reason to quake since gagmen Nat Perrin and Frank Tashlin had taken this story by Devery Freeman and hammered it into yet another showcase for the formidable Miss Ball. But Perrin and Tashlin were not quite the hammerers they thought they were, virtually splitting the movie down

DEAR WIFE (1950). With Joan Caulfield

the center in the process.

On the one hand, there is an energetic and briny rapport among Holden, Frank McHugh, and James Gleason, as the bookmaking confederates. Bacon's direction keeps step with the peppery, punch-counterpunch dialogue, sparred admirably by the threesome without line-stepping or upstaging. Then, there is the broad, typically clownish playing of Lucille Ball in her prime. Here, Bacon's direction seems impatient with the comedienne's deliberate style, rushing to pay off a sight gag or hurrying a slow joke, and giving the distinct impression that someone or something is lagging.

At its best, *Miss Grant Takes Richmond* has its seams showing but is politely accommodating to both sides. At its worst, the movie is distractingly rent, with two identities that not only fail to lock step, but often actively compete. What it amounts to is everyone doing what he or she does best, though with the high calibre of talent, things could be much worse.

Holden's work is of special note. He refuses to swerve before his awesome leading lady and mixes it with McHugh and Gleason (two of the top comedy character actors in the trade) as if weaned on the rapid-fire style of the thirties. His delivery is trimmed to the bone, and his compact comedy approach lends new truth to the less-is-more method. Holden's freshness effectively prevents *Miss Grant* from becoming just another Lucille Ball movie.

As a rule, non-serial sequels seldom become equals. Just the same, it's hard to throw studio executives off the scent of a proven property, and so few people were surprised when Paramount pulled its *Dear Ruth* formula out of mothballs, dusted it off, updated it, and resold it as *Dear Wife*.

This first of five 1950 Holden appearances was not exactly his best foot forward. The original cast and concept had been, at best, a lucky recipe, and here they were being asked to repeat that performance. The result is a cookbook movie where situations and characterizations mix with all the subtlety of labeled ingredients.

In yet another ode to the housing shortage, Holden and Joan Caulfield, now man and wife, are forced to live with her family. Minor squabbles snowball as Holden and father-in-law Edward Arnold quarrel over such weighty topics as the merits of grapefruit. Matters go from frying pan to fire when the impish younger daughter, again Mona Freeman, schemes to pit son-in-law against father-in-law in an election for State Senator. On such situational fuel as this, *Dear Wife* squeaks along to a predictably smiling conclusion. For all it did not do, the movie did make money. Enough, in fact, that in the time-honored tradition of Hollywood overkill, Paramount later issued another sequel, *Dear Brat* (1951), featuring Freeman, sans Holden and Caulfield. Their absence was their good fortune.

If *Dear Wife* had meant getting off on the wrong foot, *Father is a Bachelor* (1950) was an out-and-out stumble. Shackled with the role of Johnny Rutledge, a no-account hobo who is reactivated by a fivesome of devastatingly adorable orphans, Holden seems here to be launching his second decade in film on a wing and a prayer. This movie is the sort of maudlin mulch that brought him closest in spirit to his father's fertilizer business. With its listless and rambling story, *Father is a Bachelor* recalled for Holden the customary salvation cliché, "always darkest before the dawn." But the movie's stark bankruptcy (*Variety* called it "almost a complete waste of money and talent") was really a logical punctuation to the largely soulless string of roles with which Holden had been saddled.

An intricate individual by nature, William Holden had been repeatedly strangled by studio-assigned, cardboard cut-out parts that too often left him grinning vacantly. For him, these were chores, not choices.

FATHER IS A BACHELOR (1950). With Warren Farlow, Gary Gray, Wayne Farlow, Billy Gray, Mary Jane Saunders, and Coleen Gray

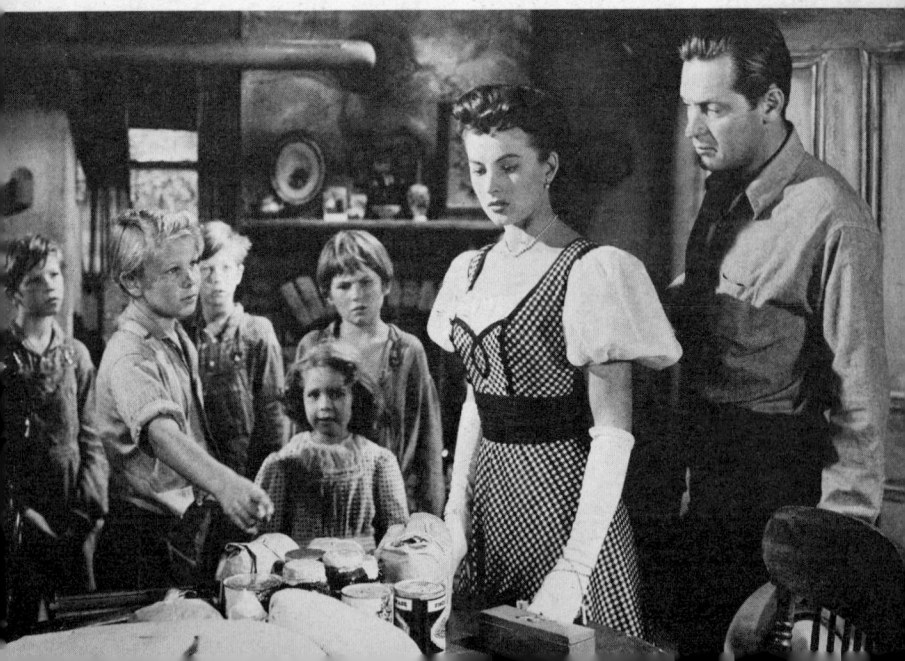

"The first thing I think of before accepting a part is the quality of the production, not the role. Maybe I've been fortunate."—to *United Press International*, January, 1953

APPLE PIE GONE AWRY

It was a mild, mid-April night in 1949, and the long-vacant mansion-monstrosity at the corner of Wilshire and Crenshaw Boulevards in Los Angeles was suddenly teeming with personnel and equipment. Nonchalant neighbors knew at a glance—a motion picture was being made.

In the rear lawn area of the estate, preliminary shooting had been completed and the crew was beginning to pack up for the night. His own night's work done, Bill Holden was off to one side of the grounds, finessing a cigarette and trading wisecracks with his director, Billy Wilder. Cameraman Johnny Seitz and assistant director C.C. "Buddy" Coleman appeared abruptly and headed for Wilder. The two were troubled about a brief scene on the next evening's shot list, a macabre backyard burial of a pet monkey. Coleman had no idea how to set it up and Seitz was stumped over the correct way to shoot. Wilder thought a second, fingered his cigarette, and dead-panned, "It's very simple. It's just the usual dead-chimpanzee shot." Holden knew he was working on a very unusual motion picture.

The idea for *Sunset Boulevard* (1950) had been hatched months before by Wilder and his partner Charles Brackett, with a later boost from D.M. Marshman and, in absentia, Balzac, whose *Le Père Goriot* suggested a key dramatic twist that finally got the project off the ground.

As eventually wrought, the story focuses on Joe Gillis, a young, acerbic writer of "B" movies, who is down on his luck. While eluding creditors one afternoon, he chances upon a musty, delapidated mansion, which is inhabited by a bizarrely imperious woman and her Teutonic butler, Max. After being mistaken for an animal undertaker come to bury a pet chimpanzee, Gillis turns to exit when it occurs to him that the pallid woman is Norma Desmond, one of the great silent stars who, along with many others, was unable to span the Hollywood transition to talkies. The writer bluntly remarks, "You're Norma Desmond. You used to be in pictures. You used to be big." Like queen to knave, she replies, "I *am* big. It's the movies that got small."

The stage is set. The washed-up

SUNSET BOULEVARD (1950). With Gloria Swanson

siren is planning a gala comeback in a personalized version of *Salomé*. At her request, Gillis examines the script, finding it so much scrawl, but seeing in it a chance to finagle some fast dollars. He offers to rewrite, and she accepts. Presently, she offers more than rewriting, and he accepts. The gigolo Gillis becomes our window on this out-of-kilter world of the once-greats, sating every sordid curiosity to the brink of nausea. In time, he finds the atmosphere suffocating, seeing himself all-too-really as a "ghostwriter."

With this, the plot accelerates. Gillis pursues an outside life but Norma wrenches him back with an attempted suicide. A brief lull, then he is out again, on the sly, collaborating on a film script with a young woman, proving to himself that he has gifts as a writer, as well as normal romantic impulses. Norma gets wind of the tryst and phones the girl, wickedly trying to ward her off: "Do you know where he lives? How he lives? What he lives on? He does not live with relatives, or friends in the usual sense of the word."

Gillis overhears the treachery, and the moral squalor of the entire situation repels him. He decides to return to Dayton, Ohio and his $35-a-week job at the newspaper. Norma pleads for him to stay and brandishes a pistol, again threatening suicide if he goes, but he ignores her. Impulsively, she wheels on Gillis, shooting him repeatedly as he staggers doll-like into the swimming pool, quite dead.

In its original form, the story was to have opened in a morgue, with a number of corpses chatting airily as Gillis tenders his own tale. The prologue was actually shot, previewed, and junked in favor of an opening shot of Gillis floating face down in the pool, and then flashing back on a corpse-eye view of the preceding events.

Also, originally Gillis was to be played by Montgomery Clift, who backed out a scant two weeks before shooting, fearing so shabby a character might harm his image. A jittery Billy Wilder rifled the Paramount casting lists and picked Holden, whom he remembered as a smiling, second lieutenant type. The match was made.

In pre-production, Holden seemed a small fish alongside the bravura casting of personalities that were but a half-beat away from their roles. Gloria Swanson, whose own soaring silent career was dashed upon the rocks of sound, acted, and peripherally was, the sadly ghoulish Norma Desmond. The parallels abound. At one point, Norma even does a jaunty impression of Chaplin, as Gloria Swanson had once done in *Manhandled* (1924). Yet, of the many intersections of actress and role, none is so searing as the scene in which Norma and Joe view a past Desmond feature (in fact, Miss Swanson's own *Queen Kelly* [1928] financed by her at $800,000, but never released domestically). Norma is wistfully watching her young actress self when an intense close-up and title insertion, "Cast out this wicked dream that has seized my heart," cause her to fume and leap to her feet. With the flickering projector shedding a ghastly stroboscopic light on her face, she exclaims, "Have they forgotten what a star looks like? I'll be up there again, so help me." Just how much of herself Gloria Swanson deliberately invested in that scene is open to debate, but it is the lone buffer between a daring performance and cruel self-parody.

The second casting coup is in the role of Max Von Meyerling, the butler and chauffeur who, it is later divulged, had been the maverick director first to ignite Norma's career. Erich von Stroheim, himself the prodigal silent director whose eccentric genius doomed his career, played Max with a wincing empathy. It was, moreover, von Stroheim who had directed the excerpted *Queen Kelly*.

There are other overlappings of fact and fiction, but these become trivial and only deflect from the film's intrinsic worth. That is where Holden enters. He is an actor among superstars, a man among myths, and his Joe Gillis is the pivotal role which prevents the picture from becoming a "who's who" of industry washouts. His hand-in-pocket manner and spare gestures create a necessary axis for Miss Swanson's baroque characterization. But there is more to his performance than first meets the eye.

As the film's narrator, Holden's voice is caustic and colloquial, intelligent and wry, with none of the recital vanity common to many actors trained in speech. On screen, he aptly weaves Gillis' dualistic personality as the innocent midwesterner and the parasitic, self-hating hack. His face is scrubbed and his hair groomed, but his smile is noticeably awry and his eyes darting and inward-looking. He is indispensably flexible in parrying Miss Swanson's ravenous advances while cueing the much-needed romantic relief with Nancy Olson. William Holden is *Sunset Boulevard*'s underplayed pacer, its rhythm. At age thirty-one, he gives a tour de force performance.

For reasons best known to Brackett and Wilder, the film was shelved for over a year and not generally released until August of 1950. The delay did nothing to dull its impact or stall the stir it caused within the industry and without. The film netted Oscar nominations

SUNSET BOULEVARD (1950). With Nancy Olson

SUNSET BOULEVARD (1950). With Gloria Swanson

down the line, but in most categories lost to Joseph L. Mankiewicz's coincidental theater counterpart, *All About Eve*. Holden pulled up short for best actor honors to Jose Ferrer's *Cyrano de Bergerac,* but the loss was incidental beside the other gains. Of far greater worth, he had forged a friendship with Billy Wilder based on mutual professional esteem, and had attained critical stature, showing himself an actor of the first water.

There was a new and fascinating Holden forming off screen as well, or at least, so thought the press which was peering belatedly past its own star-blinded copy into the man behind the actor. Holden was praised as one of Hollywood's leading citizens for devoting much personal time to community causes. On the board of the Screen Actors Guild, he had helped chair the Veterans Affairs Committee, which actively sought work for returning actor war veterans, particularly supporting and bit players. As a member of the Motion Pictures Industry Council, he later served on the Permanent Charities Committee, and, in an honorary post, became the Commissioner of Parks and Recreation for Los Angeles. Holden's most substantial contribution was to the Screen Actors Guild, where he rose to the posi-

SUNSET BOULEVARD (1950). With Gloria Swanson and Anna Q. Nilsson

UNION STATION (1950). As Lieut. William Calhoun

BORN YESTERDAY (1950). With Judy Holliday and Broderick Crawford

tion of Vice President and bargained stubbornly and cunningly on behalf of actors.

Voluntary work aside, Bill Holden was not grovelling with gratitude over the apparent upswing in his career. This was clearest in his reaction to resurgent attention from the press, which was fast admitting that there was more to this man than a smile and a laundered family life. There was much talk of a publicity debt to his loyal public, but Holden would have none of it. In an interview with *Photoplay,* he set the ground rules as he saw them. "What the public expects is sometimes what the actor considers an invasion of privacy. I owe my success to guys like Billy Wilder. Popularity is due to good pictures."

Holden's candor ruffled the temperamental fan rags and he was tagged a hostile ingrate, biting the hand that headlined him. In a second interview, he tried to clarify his position as to privacy. "I've tried to keep my nose clean in my dealings with the press, so I guess it has paid off because they haven't hit me below the belt very often." Qualifying that double-edged concession further, he added, "I came to the conclusion that if reporters didn't want to write about me without references to my family, they needn't write about me." He was on the record, and the reactionary local tattlers were in a quandary over the whereabouts of the gosh-and-golly golden boy of a decade ago.

Swept in on the wave of *Sunset Boulevard*'s reputation, *Union Station* opened to large crowds in the fall of 1950. An unspectacular drama about a kidnapping within the jurisdiction of railway police, it lacks the precision and style of a fine detective piece. Much of the problem is Sydney Boehm's dialogue, by no means crackling. But neither is Rudolph Maté's atmospheric direction very mobile. Nor, for that matter, is the teaming of Holden and Nancy Olson as sizzling as might have been expected after their romanticus interruptus in *Sunset Boulevard*.

Briefly, the plot dwells on the train station abduction of the blind daughter of a local tycoon, as witnessed by Miss Olson. She, in turn, notifies transit cop Holden, who wades into the investigation with his menacing goon squad and suspiciously priestly Inspector, Barry Fitzgerald. Several corpses and red-herrings later, Holden locates and corners the manic murderer-kidnapper (played maniacally and murderously by Lyle Bettger), gunning him down in a dingy railroad tunnel, as the rattled daughter is returned unharmed to dad. Hurdling the stiff plotting and the hackneyed dialogue ("A cop can't be sentimental,") Holden displays a certain flare for the detective style. He makes a credible cop, and dispenses a kidney-punch and a kiss with comparable ease.

Without breaking stride, Holden strolled into the filming of the celebrated Garson Kanin play, *Born Yesterday* (1950). Judy Holliday, the peerless comic actress who had immortalized the play's focal role of Billie Dawn on stage in over 1,600 performances, had been signed to repeat the role on screen. Holden hankered for a major part in the film, and the happy result was his teaming with Miss Holliday. George Cukor was asked to direct, and Broderick Crawford (with his 1949 Oscar for *All the King's Men*) was added for billing strength.

The film, extremely faithful to the play, tells of a crude junkyard magnate, Harry Brock, who comes to Washington with his brassy, ex-chorine mistress, Billie Dawn, to buy off a few politicians en route to forming a cartel of dubious legality. Harry is as pained by Billie's earthiness as he is proud of his own, and employs Paul Verrall, a local hard-nosed investigative reporter, to see her through some mental calisthenics. The scheme curdles when Billie's vacuity yields to an eager, childlike curiosity, sensing something is amiss in Harry's pending manipulations. This is a chilling development for Harry, who, for

BORN YESTERDAY (1950). With Judy Holliday

FORCE OF ARMS (1951). With Nancy Olson

SUBMARINE COMMAND (1952). With Don Taylor and William Bendix

tax purposes, has made his paramour the legal owner of over half his holdings. The story wends its polemical path, playing democratic idealism against capitalistic corruption, and bringing matters to a crunching finale wherein Billie extorts a vow of honesty from Harry and wangles a vow of marriage from Paul.

The acting is roundly excellent, even to the point of smoothing isolated textual and directorial rough spots. Crawford seizes the role of Brock (played on stage by Paul Douglas), hardening and coarsening it, yet leaving the tiniest shred of brutish sympathy. As Paul Verrall (originated by Gary Merrill), Holden is cuttingly reserved, avoiding caricature by particularizing the character. The role is deceivingly difficult, since it is a key foil for Billie Dawn's comic wordplay and bluntness. Holden makes a superb straight man as the crusading intellectual, while retaining virility, if not sheer sexiness.

But the show-stopping performance is Miss Holliday's Billie Dawn, played with a surgical precision and raucous charm unique among comic actresses. That talent won her the year's Oscar over a superlative field of actresses, not least of whom was Gloria Swanson. It looked as if William Holden was acquiring a knack for showing his leading ladies to good advantage.

Born Yesterday was not long out

BOOTS MALONE (1952). With Basil Ruysdael and Stanley Clements

of the gates when it was provided with an ironic footnote. William H. Mooring, syndicated critic for a number of regional Catholic newspapers, assailed the film as subversive leftist propaganda, "satire strictly from Marx," continuing, "Never have human symbols been more subtly molded to carry destructive comment through disarming comedy." The red-baiting went so far as boycotts in New York and New Jersey by two chapters of Catholic War Veterans. Many rushed to the film's defense, chiefly Kenneth Clark of the Motion Picture Association of America. The commotion deflated and did not visibly hamper the film's returns. Neither, for that matter, did the domestic ranks of the Communist Party swell in its wake.

The accusations tickled Holden, who had recently donated his services to a mildly anti-Communist two-reeler that was making the rounds regionally. Called *You Can Change the World* (1950), and directed by Leo McCarey, it had been conceived and engineered by Father James Keller, organizer of the Christopher's Unit of the Roman Catholic Church. The film presented some dozen Hollywood stars in a sometimes humorous running dialogue on our slackening moral fiber.

In the wash of Hollywood's attenuated replaying of the Second

World War, Holden made a pair of movies that seemed pressed from almost identical molds. Both *Force of Arms* (1951) and *Submarine Command* (1952) teamed him with the fast-wilting Nancy Olson, placed him under crusty, experienced directors, and cast him as a junior officer forced to sacrifice his ranking officer in combat for the greater good of the outfit.

Michael Curtiz' *Force of Arms* was set in Italy and was highlighted by a number of gritty, skillfully staged battle sequences. As the conscience-stricken first lieutenant, Holden is spare and splintery, struggling within to find whether romance has made him less a soldier. The answer arrives resoundingly in a final redemptive episode instructing that heroism and love are not mutually exclusive enterprises.

As if to see whether the proposition really holds water, *Submarine Command* has Commander Holden abandoning his wounded Skipper topside during an enemy attack. He again grapples with the shadings of duty, as the doubts persist and scuff his marriage. Unlike the previous struggle, resolution is a full war away, but Korea gives the submariner a stage for revival, played out in a desperate rescue operation. In his first work with director John Farrow since the rickety *Blaze of Noon*, Holden responds well in this action tale that is deft, though clearly derivative.

Accepting a brief suspension from Paramount, Holden hoped to lodge a protest over what he took to be flat material. The complaints fell on the deaf ears of studio executives, who simply extended the terms of his contract commensurate with his absence. Such were the fortunes of servitude.

The skirmish lost, Holden returned to work in the first of two consecutive films directed by William Dieterle. *Boots Malone* (1952) is an unsentimental account of a boy's entrance into the world of horse racing. It is shot with an eye to detail and authenticity, and brims with racetrack lore. Holden is handed the title role and, in what can be best described as a generous walkthrough, scowls and grimaces along as an unscrupulous jockey's agent whose malice is diluted, though never fully dissolved, by young runaway Johnny Stewart.

The film is soundly acted and the direction unflagging, never once stooping to process shots or other artifice. *Boots Malone* is genuine and rugged, but could have benefited from well-placed light touches as relief from its relentless abrasiveness.

The second half of this Dieterle double is *The Turning Point* (1952), a johnny-come-lately topical thriller rising in the dust of Senator

THE TURNING POINT (1952). With Edmond O'Brien and Alexis Smith

Kefauver's investigations into organized crime. Holden is a dauntless, gun-toting reporter who, on request, throws in with friend and Chief Investigator Edmond O'Brien, as they attempt to get the goods on local syndicate king-pin Ed Begley. There is a measure of triangular romance, as well, in the person of Alexis Smith, O'Brien's girlfriend-secretary who becomes enamored of Holden. In the end, the rackets get busted, and Holden dusted by a hired gunman, leaving the headlines and Miss Smith to O'Brien.

In his last four feature appearances, William Holden had handled successive opaque parts with a typed posturing, a lumpish personality whom he knowingly and derisively called "Disgruntled Dan." Holden was coasting on that image when he faced a career crossroad. Billy Wilder had acquired the rights to *Stalag 17*, a play by Donald Bevan and Edmund Trzcinski about life in a German prisoner of war camp during World War II. The production had enjoyed a solid Broadway run, but, if unusual for its conception, it had been unremarkable in its execution.

Working with Edwin Blum, Wilder set about expanding the piece into a screenplay, doctoring and dismantling it. When casting began in January of 1952, the major parts had been so altered that it was understood only a handful of

STALAG 17 (1953). As Sefton

STALAG 17 (1953). With Sig Ruman

STALAG 17 (1953). With Don Taylor

the stage players would still be suitable. By far, the most difficult spot to fill was that of Sergeant Sefton, as rewritten, a singular, somewhat paradoxical character requiring almost molecular acting sensitivity. Wilder first considered a callow Charlton Heston, but quickly hedged on the choice. With the start of shooting closing fast, the director turned to the actor who had bailed him out once before, William Holden.

After a string of "Disgruntled Dans," this role initially seemed cut from the same cloth. Sefton was brooding, isolated, and gnawingly inscrutable. By the same token, he was a gutsy loner, sardonic, and entirely his own man. It might be a blanket caricature, and then, it might be a tricky and challenging skin to get under. Holden was enticed. After all, Wilder was a man whose judgment he trusted. He accepted the role.

Stalag 17 (1953) started shooting in February, 1952 and wound up well ahead of schedule the following month. There was a casual camaraderie on the set, with the seasoned Broadway supporting hands, Robert Strauss, Harvey Lembeck, and William Pierson, orienting the Hollywood latecomers, Richard Erdman, Neville Brand, Peter Graves, and Don Taylor. Otto Preminger had been drafted as an actor for the occasion, and even author Trzcinski pocketed some screen time as an extra.

The central plot runs much as it had on stage. Set the week before Christmas in 1944, it opens on a thwarted escape attempt from Stalag 17, the fleeing inmates getting machine-gunned for their trouble. Tempers flare back at the barracks where Sefton, playing the odds above and beyond sentiment, has made book against the escape. (No prisoner has ever left Stalag 17 alive.) When news of the deaths filters back, Sefton is accused of tipping the guards for personal gain.

Accusations mount as more prisoner secrets find their way into the hands of the Camp Commandant. When classified news of successful sabotage by a recent captive leaks to the Germans, the mood of the prisoners takes a brutal turn. Sefton, the most likely fall guy, is assumed to be the informer and thrashed mercilessly by his barracks mates. Hoping to clear himself and avenge his beating, the cuffed outcast coolly sniffs out the actual informer. In a tense, last-minute unmasking, Sefton pegs the barracks security chief as a Nazi plant, and, using him as diversionary bait to the guards, engineers a successful escape with the prisoner-saboteur. The other prisoners marvel at their own

Holding his Oscar for Best Actor for STALAG 17

ruthless wrongmindedness, as Sefton departs, character intact.

Wilder fleshes out this skeletal story with several beautifully designed vignettes highlighting Sefton's game ingenuity. There is the running of the Stalag 17 Turf Club, literally a rat race, with cigarettes as currency and Sefton figuring the tote board odds. There is also the periodic running of an improvised still, where "all the house guarantees is you don't go blind." But Wilder's handiest innovation is the creation of a third person narrator, Sefton's adoring lackey, Cookie (Gil Stratton, Jr.), who unfurls the story suspensefully, almost like a detective mystery.

At the character level, the film is exquisite. Lembeck and Strauss transport their broad stage buffoonery as Harry and Stosh, Sig Ruman adds a clownish touch as Schulz, the jolly prison guard acting as courier between informant and commandant. Otto Preminger's commandant lists slightly toward exaggeration, but Peter Graves' fair-haired Nazi informer is an inspired bit of casting for offbeat villainy. Yet it takes Holden's Sefton to keep this from becoming just another rogues' gallery.

At Wilder's suggestion, Holden's hair was cropped to suede length, and with the vindictive bruising inflicted early in the film, his Sefton wears a shiner and a nasty gash below the left eye through most of the footage. Slouch-shouldered, five o'clock-shadowed, and head cocked sassily to the side, the usually wholesome Holden dons the vampiric visage of a scornful opportunist. Against this exterior, the actor molds a character interior that is both more and less than face value.

As first written and portrayed on stage by John Ericson, Sefton was strictly knowable, embittered, but eager to prove his patriotism in a pinch. Holden's Sefton is far more colorful and enigmatic. He is decidedly his own man, following a highly personal code of ethics. He is raspy, sarcastic, and egocentric—a peculiarly American, cigar-puffing, small-time robber-baron who thrives on adversity and uses his gruff image as a foil for the resolute man of honor beneath the surface. His memorable exit tells it all. Sefton has cleared himself of blame, and is about to slip out of the barracks' trap door toward escape, when he pauses for a farewell. Fixing his compatriots with a smoldering gaze, he warns, "If I ever run into any of you bums on a streetcorner, just let's pretend we never met before." With that, he vanishes, but reappears a moment later. Smiling crookedly, he tips his hat and is gone.

Once again, Wilder closeted his film, this time a full sixteen months until July of 1953. And, as before, acclaim was fast in coming. Holden had proven himself a mighty actor, performing with an intriguing stylistic thrift befitting the character. His rendition of Sefton was classic. He knew it. Wilder knew it. And, at last, the Academy of Motion Picture Arts and Sciences knew it, awarding Holden the Oscar for best actor.

And to think it had all started face down in a swimming pool.

"I work for a living. Certainly I enjoy my work and I get paid for it, but I'm as much in business as the corner druggist."

—to *Cue* Magazine, April, 1954

PAVING THE ROAD TO KWAI

The Oscar was consecrated with the familiar fanfare and fireworks. But when the smoke cleared, there was William Holden, smiling a different smile. For him, it had all been anticlimax. The award simply sealed and certified something he had long since grasped—that purist acting was not a realistic goal within the Hollywood system. An actor was just an actor, but a star was a commodity. With the Oscar as his price tag, Holden was not only ready to be that commodity, he was determined to manage and market it himself.

Of course, he was not brash enough to think he could buck the studio entirely. He had seen too many peers parlay autonomy into anonymity. Holden was bent on finding his freedom within the system, and with the specter of television already looming ominously on the horizon, Hollywood was uncharacteristically open-minded on the subject.

Holden began by renegotiating his contract with Paramount. The new terms called for twenty-eight films to be made at the rate of at least two per year, at an annual salary of $250,000. There was an important provision for independent outside projects, plus an option to work through the Paramount quota more quickly if desired. The businessman Holden had obtained what the actor Holden had earned—security and leeway. Which is not to imply that acting had been cast into the hinterlands.

Stalag 17 had marked a temporary plateau. Holden felt that he had surveyed a personal dramatic repertoire and was content, for the time, to grow within those boundaries. Independence was to be signaled hastily with an innocuous property, *The Moon is Blue* (1953). As actor and backer, Holden threw in with Otto Preminger, his snarling co-star of *Stalag 17,* who had first produced this F. Hugh Herbert play on Broadway. From the outset, the watchword was profit.

With an accountant's eye to the foreign markets, director Preminger filmed two versions at once. A scene would first be shot with the American cast of Holden, David Niven, Maggie McNamara and Dawn Addams, then the German cast of Hardy Kruger, Johannes Heesters, and Johanna

THE MOON IS BLUE (1953). With Maggie McNamara, David Niven, and Dawn Addams

Matz, would trot through the same material. Historically, this was the first bilingual Hollywood production since MGM's *Merry Widow* in 1934. More history was yet to be made.

The Moon is Blue is essentially a flirty little morality play. It concerns a bachelor on the make (Holden) who makes the acquaintance of a young actress (Maggie McNamara), trying to make it in New York but unwilling to be made in the process. The girl is guardedly, even boastfully virginal, and blabs about it candidly and endlessly. A lecherous neighbor (Niven) descends on the scene, voicing

THE MOON IS BLUE (1953). With Maggie McNamara

motley chaste-makes-waste philosophies before succumbing to the girl's sanitary charm. The pseudo-sophisticated byplay dips to sophomoric banter, as things lope to a prim conclusion that finds the original bachelor suitor proposing marriage to this overgrown bobby-soxer actress.

The acting is uniformly dispirited, save for Miss McNamara, who tries her best to be a coyly domestic Audrey Hepburn. But the real drama occurred off screen, where the film came under fire for its offhand use of the word "virgin." As if out of a sense of monopoly on virginity, the Catholic Legion of Decency condemned *The Moon is Blue* and the Breen Office followed suit by denying it the Production Code Seal.

Out of equal parts indignity and greed, Preminger offered to go to court, throwing the entire scandal into bold headlines. On the strength of such newsy publicity, he decided instead to go into release in defiance of the Production Code, stating "I believe that it is my right to offer it to the public intact, for the public's verdict." Launched by the mystique of the forbidden, the film did a land-office business, meeting with only intermittent bans and bluff obscenity charges. The public verdict was approval, with doubt over the morality fuss. Abroad, where the film was released as *Die Jungfrau Auf Dem*

FOREVER FEMALE (1954). With Paul Douglas and Ginger Rogers

Dach ("The Virgin on the Roof"), audiences might just as easily been watching Bugs Bunny.

The commotion fell as sharply as it had risen, and, as the saying goes, Preminger and Holden shrugged all the way to the bank.

Far less profitable was Holden's first chore under his new contract, *Forever Female* (1954). Writers Julius and Phillip Epstein had taken their inspiration from a slender J.M. Barrie one-act play, *Rosalind*, which they repackaged as a flabby screenplay about an actress who learns under duress to act her own age. Holden's characterization of an arrogant but gifted young playwright is the only sleek item amid wavering excesses of every kind.

Ginger Rogers is the aging actress, Beatrice Page, who fights for—then sadly surrenders—the opportunity to play the young lead in a promising maiden work by Stanley Krown (Holden). But Miss Rogers has trouble handling her accent as Page (ranging from fractured Queen's English, to Fifth Avenue, to Broadway chippie) let alone her character, and the bearish Paul Douglas is no help as her producer and former husband. Worse yet is the ingenue Pat Crowley, as the ingenue Sally Carver, who hounds the playwright for the lead. Miss Crowley plays to the rafters without fail, carries on a brazen dalliance with the camera, and throws herself into each scene like a grenade.

Irving Rapper's direction does nothing to shear the excess, and the Epstein brothers' dialogue does everything to aggravate it. As behind-the-scenes theater drama, it's all been said before, and been said better. After back-to-back balloons (one hot air, the other lead), Holden was ready to get his feet back on the ground.

He escaped to *Escape From Fort Bravo* (1954), his first brush with MGM. Back in uniform as a Captain in the Union Cavalry, he is the stern warden of Confederate prisoners at a frontier outpost in Arizona. Eleanor Parker is the pretty poison in league with the rebels, acting as decoy for their successful escape. Holden gives chase and catches up to them moments before a band of marauding Mescalero Indians catches up to them all. From then on, it is like a soup made with twenty favorite Western ingredients, all the way down to the hollowly heroic end and the onrushing cavalry. The only novelty is the Indian siege, in which the Mescaleros shower arrows with the tactical know-how of a modern-day mortar attack. Beyond that, director John Sturges brings nothing new to the setting.

It was only a short step back to the present and *Executive Suite*

ESCAPE FROM FORT BRAVO (1954). With Eleanor Parker and Richard Anderson

EXECUTIVE SUITE (1954). With June Allyson

(1954). Based on the novel by Cameron Hawley, the Robert Wise-directed film tells of the clawing scramble for corporate power when an autocratic chairman of the board dies unexpectedly with no heir apparent in the company. While hardly a glib indictment of corporate politics, *Executive Suite* does point up the ruthless maneuvering that takes place behind closed doors in tall buildings.

The narrative bounces around, busily trying to keep tabs on the assorted candidates for replacement, and might have collapsed into chaos were it not for the polished acting of the distinguished cast. Fredric March, Barbara Stanwyck, Walter Pidgeon, Louis Calhern, Dean Jagger, and Holden keep the story's machinery running, but the necessary spottiness of a top-heavy production makes it all resemble a treadmill.

As the altruistic, technocratic company man, William Holden is *Executive Suite*'s best lubricant, his character's struggle being the main source of movement. The performance, which peaks in a fiery speech before the assembled board, is powerfully convincing, nourished

EXECUTIVE SUITE (1954). With Nina Foch, Barbara Stanwyck, Walter Pidgeon, Dean Jagger, Louis Calhern, and Fredric March

by the actor's triple incentive. For one, the film's message spoke for Holden's own ideals of corporate integrity. For another, this was his first work with Barbara Stanwyck since *Golden Boy,* and he was anxious to show his mentor how well he had ironed the wrinkles in his acting. But above all, the performance reflected Holden's wish to do credit to his co-star, March, whom he had always worshipped as an actor.

A slight tumble was coming, however, and it was coming where least expected—in a third collaboration with Billy Wilder. Not to break with his pattern, Holden was once more a late entry. Wilder had obtained the Samuel Taylor play, *Sabrina Fair* (shortened to *Sabrina* for the 1954 film) about a scrawny chauffeur's daughter who blossoms into an enchanting young woman, beguiling the two sons of her father's wealthy employer. Cary Grant was asked to play the older of the filial pair, Linus, a part written for mature but spry elegance. When Grant refused, the part was turned over to Humphrey Bogart, certainly mature, though neither spry nor elegant. Some compensatory casting was in order for Linus' younger brother David, the much-married playboy, and Holden got the call. With Audrey Hepburn ideally cast in the Cinderella title role and lending marquee power after her Oscar for *Roman Holiday*

SABRINA (1954). With Audrey Hepburn

SABRINA (1954). With Audrey Hepburn

(1953) (adding to the recent Oscars of her two co-stars), Wilder estimated that the obvious age disparity and miscasting would be forgotten. He was wrong.

Bogart looks fatigued and bored. He plays his comedy with a vengeance and all but drives the breezy plot into the ground. Light, patrician romance is not his forte, and as for age, even his character says, "Look at me, Joe College with a touch of arthritis." Holden does no better by the idiocy of the brattish, skylarking David, but unlike Bogart, he trustingly gives himself over to the role, by his later appraisal, "one of the most difficult I ever had." It is a gamble that lands on its face, like a laughless pratfall.

Whatever the toll in actor's pride, a wide path is cleared for the willowy Miss Hepburn, and she glides along like music. The film is handsomely mounted by Wilder and stunningly photographed by Charles Lang, Jr.. Visually, it is like a black tuxedo that sets off Hepburn's evening gown character. And Wilder, Bogart, and Holden could not seem less at home.

But then, directors like to think of themselves as sorcerers, and if Wilder had failed to make a juvenile of a fine actor, George Seaton was no less willing to try to make a dramatic actor of a crooner. Bing Crosby set aside his "buhbuhbuh boos" and took the lead in the 1954 film version of Clifford Odets' *The Country Girl*. As Frank Elgin, he plays a musical-comedy star on the skids, wallowing in alcohol and self-pity. Also cast against type, Grace Kelly is his shopworn wife, homely and sullen, by turns coddling and tyrannizing her drunkard husband. Cast more to type, Holden plays stage director Bernie Dodd, who wants to restore Elgin to the stage, and thus, to self-respect.

With Dodd's push stopping just short of shove, Elgin finally makes his comeback, but only after the director has learned that Mrs. Elgin's shrewish ways come of the many years she has had to serve as backbone for her mealy-mouthed husband. A romance flickers between Mrs. Elgin and Dodd but it is doused in an opening-night cocktail party confessional where Elgin admits his past wretchedness and his wife decides to see him through the final leg of recuperation. The director Dodd remains the unsung hero, the most solitary of his kind since Warner Baxter's fade-out over two decades earlier in *42nd Street*.

Crosby's performance was hailed as courageous and moving. The truth of the matter is that he remains a glum centerpiece while Kelly and Holden act circles around him. His emotional range is

THE COUNTRY GIRL (1954). With Grace Kelly

limited and so lumbering that it is often out of sync dramatically. Not bad for a crooner, but certainly not up to the standard set by Miss Kelly. Her early line, "I'm just a girl from the country" does not especially strike home (she sounds as countrified as caviar), but from that point on, she is doggedly in step with her character.

Holden, meanwhile, brings off another demanding role, vitalizing a somewhat stock character and offering an elastic dramatic counterpoint to both Crosby and Kelly. Holden knew the ropes too well to think fine performances could exist in a vacuum. When Grace Kelly was awarded the Oscar that year, he understood that he had assisted well beyond ceremonious nods.

Audiences sometimes get what they want even before they know what they want. The on-screen electricity between Holden and Kelly was barely a memory when the two were back together in *The Bridges at Toko-Ri* (1955), playing husband and wife. They make a remarkably handsome pair, but, frankly, sparked more out of wedlock than in. Still, the match is merely a side attraction to this stinging saga of modern warfare, taken from a James Michener novel.

Holden is a Navy fighter pilot who, despite duty in the Second World War, is called back into action in Korea. He grudgingly finds

THE COUNTRY GIRL (1954). With Bing Crosby and Grace Kelly

THE BRIDGES AT TOKO-RI (1955). With Grace Kelly

LOVE IS A MANY-SPLENDORED THING (1955). With Jennifer Jones

himself leaving a wife and child to fight a war of questionable strategy in a country he's never heard of. When assigned a harrowing mission to bomb bridges deep in enemy territory, Holden senses fate closing on him like a noose. True to his intuition, his plane is downed, dumping him in a squalid irrigation ditch, where he is killed by Communist ground troops.

The Bridges at Toko-Ri is an unconventional war film that cuts to the paradoxical marrow of Cold War thinking. Its battleground is more ideological than tactical (no enemy soldier is even visible until the final reel). There is no real victory or defeat, only a costly stalemate.

The film has its conventional lapses with the spunky, brawling Mickey Rooney and occasional talk of the "Commies," and one gently instructive scene at a Tokyo public bath where we learn that the Japanese are no longer America's Oriental foe. Otherwise, the film refuses to stray. The aerial and second unit photography is impeccable, and Mark Robson's direction accurately depicts the human and inhuman sides of mechanized, modern warfare. Fredric March is helpful as a feeling, fatherly Admiral.

But the film belongs to Holden, whose reluctant warrior does not exit in a heroic, patriotic blaze. He is mortal to the end, not an idea but

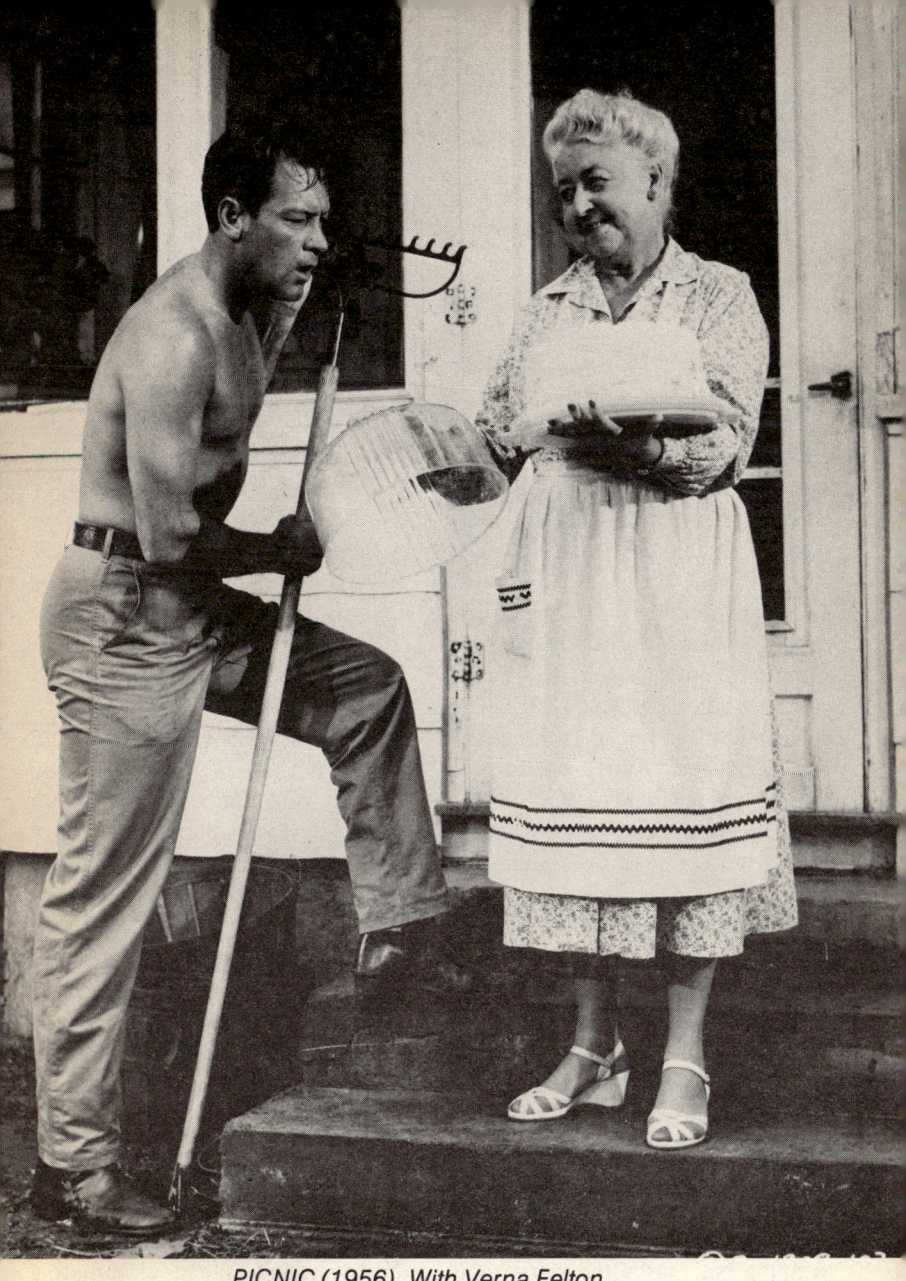
PICNIC (1956). With Verna Felton

a dead man in a mudhole. For those who knew of the death of Holden's brother, Bob, under like circumstances, the portrayal was deeply touching.

Less so was his turn in Henry King's *Love is a Many-Splendored Thing* (1955), which is as close as William Holden has ever come to soap opera. Not to say that this is purely sudsy fare. Based on the novel by Han Suyin, who took her title from Francis Thompson's poem, *The Kingdom of God,* this story of love between a dedicated Eurasian doctor (Jennifer Jones) and a cynical war correspondent (Holden) owes much to classic romance. It does not gush cheap sentimentality, but is soft-spoken and aphoristic, nearly poetic in a number of sequences. Of course, when it misses its mark, which is often, the dialogue does slide into bargain-basement Buddhism that reads like the inside of a fortune cookie. The film is saved from choppiness by the steady acting of Holden and Miss Jones, who manage to wax romantic without too much unsightly lather.

Love's only lingering weakness comes wholly from misguided production values which try to make a maudlin tearjerker of the sensitive tale. Sammy Fain's Oscar-winning but mushy theme swirls in and out like a typhoon, almost spoiling the crucial moment when Miss Jones learns of Holden's death in Korea. Critics nuzzled the film and teasingly tagged it a "woman's movie," while they quietly dabbed at their eyes with Kleenex.

Billy Wilder had once remarked about Holden, "He doesn't put on a mask the way Lon Chaney used to do, and play a monster one day and a bedbug the next. He grew, and his growth was a healthy thing." Growth was fine, but age was more to the point when Holden accepted the youthful part of Hal Carter for a filming of William Inge's *Picnic* (1956). At thirty-seven, he had the athletic physique of a man half his age, but his face had begun to crease, and the boyish features had begun to sag. Director Joshua Logan, who had guided Ralph Meeker through the part on Broadway, thought Holden could handle the difficulties. He was not disappointed.

Set in a mid-Kansas whistle-stop, the story opens on Labor Day morning, as the townsfolk primp and prepare for the gala annual picnic. At the nearby railyards, a penniless Carter arrives by freight car, hoping to track down an old college roommate, Alan Benson, and find work with Benson's bluenose father. But the trampish Carter has the mysterious talent of radiating virility, and before any serious thought can be paid to employ-

PICNIC (1956). With Kim Novak

ment, he has mesmerized a goodly portion of the town's repressed female population, from schoolgirl to geriatric, including Benson's voluptuous girlfriend, Madge Owens. Tensions build and explode that night at the picnic as Carter openly seduces Madge in an indelibly narcotic, bluesy jazz dance. Outmanned, the jilted Benson has Carter run out of town on trumped-up charges of auto theft. But not before Hal and Madge realize they are one another's only hope for salvation from the demeaning adoration of others. Hal hurriedly hops the next freight out of town while Madge packs and busses off to meet him.

The Inge play had been designed for a smothering realism, and Logan's lushly crowded direction suits it perfectly. The film does tend to literalize much of the implied sexuality with some indelicate phallic imagery, but the photography by James Wong Howe is so sumptuously on target, and the acting of the cast so captivating, that Logan's occasional self-consciousness is forgivable.

Heading the supporting cast, Rosalind Russell plays a spinsterly, desperate schoolteacher who, fired by Holden's virile presence, forces her easy-going beau (Arthur O'Connell) to marry her. Cliff Robertson makes a believable

THE PROUD AND THE PROFANE (1956). With Deborah Kerr

gilded collegian, though Susan Strasberg is less so as Madge's ugly duckling younger sister.

Undaunted by the fact that Betty Field (as Mrs. Owens) had been a contemporary in the Paramount Golden Circle, and that he was now cast to roughly half her age, Holden tackles his role earnestly. Acting with his entire body and crafting a careful mosaic of a bewildered and jaded boy wonder, he effectively shaves years off his age. What is more, his characterization has such sweep that it carries the inexperienced Kim Novak (as Madge), who wisely plays off Holden's studied cues. The two make a lusty pair, though it's a toss up for the more photogenic chest.

As if to put quick distance between himself and the rigors of Broadway via Hollywood, Holden leaped back into uniform in George Seaton's groping World War Two melodrama, *The Proud and the Profane* (1956). Here, he is a Lieutenant Colonel in the Marines: mustachioed, steely eyed and close-mouthed—all the early signs of a Holden walk-through. Considering the scripted nonsense, this was all that might be asked.

Deborah Kerr plays a Red Cross nurse, driven to discover if her Marine husband died bravely in battle. Her quest is sidetracked when the testy Holden woos, seduces, and impregnates her, all in the twinkling of an eye. He then goes off on military maneuvers, as she discovers the admirable truth about her deceased husband and the awful truth about her domineering ways. After a stormy reunion with Holden, she suffers a miscarriage, resigning herself to celibacy and disgrace. However, her despoiler then returns from combat shell-shocked, deliriously repeating "forgive me." The doctors diagnose it as a temporary condition, "motor expressive aphasia," but the battalian chaplain pithily suggests that "God is making him write it on the blackboard 500 times." Miss Kerr revives her affection for Holden, who is in his hospital bed still blithering about forgiveness, the apparent lesson being that of such things as abject guilt and shell shock, love is made.

As was the mid-fifties vogue, Holden joined the ranks of actor-producers and formed Toluca Productions, whose first and last motion picture was *Toward the Unknown* (1956). Holden starred and Lloyd Nolan was featured in this shaky jet-age-fiction about Air Force test flying. The story, a pilot's attempt to return to active duty after a torturous spell in a Korean P.O.W. camp, is spun without conviction. Likewise, Holden, doubling as executive producer on the project, is clearly distracted in his acting as the

TOWARD THE UNKNOWN (1956). With Lloyd Nolan

tormented pilot. There is a tacky look to it all, cheapened further by the "Warnercolor" tinting, which seems to coat everything with strawberry sauce.

The most that can be said of the film is that it claims some exciting aerial work with the generous assistance of the Air Force. The real stars are not the actors, but the aircraft, X-2 and XF-120, in their screen debut.

If Holden learned anything from this abortive production venture, it was to grab a slice of the returns while leaving the headaches to others. That is precisely what he did in his next film appearance. The fact that the film was the prodigious moneymaker, *The Bridge On the River Kwai* (1957), guaranteed to fill the family coffers for generations to come, parceling 10% of the profits in $50,000 annuities. Holden could have done far worse, especially since his character hadn't even existed in early drafts of the story.

The Bridge On the River Kwai is a pseudo-historical war epic from a screenplay by Pierre Boulle, based on his own pseudo-historical novel, *The Bridge Over the River Kwai*. Boulle was a popular exponent of existentialist philosophy, and he intended to pen a condemnation of the futile madness of war. He had taken as his metaphor the actual construction of the Bangkok-Burma Railway and key bridges, by the forced labor of natives and British prisoners of war, at an astonishingly high toll to each. Whereas the factual railway was ultimately destroyed by Allied bombers and natural erosion, the novel focuses upon a single, fictional bridge, marked for sabotage by a daring team of commandos. The conflict pares down to a final confrontation between the saboteurs and the rigidly perfectionist prisoner Colonel, who first supervised the bridge project as a morale builder for his men, but has lost sight of its strategic purpose in the Japanese war effort. With the demented Colonel's interference, the mission fails and the bridge remains.

THE BRIDGE ON THE RIVER KWAI (1957). With Jack Hawkins

THE BRIDGE ON THE RIVER KWAI (1957). With Andre Morrell

THE BRIDGE ON THE RIVER KWAI (1957). With Jack Hawkins and Geoffrey Horne

Mindful of Hollywood expediencies, Boulle agreed to a pair of radical changes in the text. For one, since the characters were all either British and Japanese and neither nationality had a top box-office star at the time, a part was added to be filled by an American of sound dollar stature. For the other, Boulle was persuaded that audiences would feel cheated were the bridge left standing at the conclusion, and that it could be destroyed without harm to his underlying moral. So, from a novel that wasn't quite true to fact, came a film that wasn't quite true to the novel.

All this was of no moment to producer Sam Spiegel (late of *The African Queen* and *On the Waterfront*) who was preoccupied with other matters. Having brought cast and crew to Ceylon for shooting, his publicity department was preparing periodic press releases on the film's progress. Relayed by journalists, these tidbits teased the public imagination and created an aura of history-in-the-making. Little wonder that audiences flocked to the film as soon as it opened.

Under David Lean's stately and patient direction, *Kwai* casts a wide net of action and idea, and serves as a backdrop for a number of memorable performances. Sessue Hayakawa is pitiably human as the boozy Japanese prison Colonel who succumbs in a prideful battle of wills with his ranking British prisoner. As that prisoner, Alec Guinness is at turns incisively fanatical, dignified, and foolishly vulnerable, blinded to reality by his grand obsession. For Guinness, the role was delectably rounded, and it resulted in an Oscar.

Holden plays a practical-minded G.I. captive, who, after estimating his dim chances of survival as a prisoner, blunders through a nearly impossible escape, only to be coerced back into action as an expedition guide for the British commandos plotting to destroy the bridge. While absent from much of the footage, Holden exactly profiles this unwilling hero whose warrior instincts prove superior to those of the windy militarists with whom he is surrounded.

Yet, true to the pre-release publicity, the bridge is the main attraction, all one hundred yards long and six stories high. Even though it is disposed of in rather nebulous fashion, with Guinness first thwarting, then causing the mined explosion by conveniently dropping dead on the detonator, the event is spectacular, as the bridge collapses, taking an actual locomotive with it. Boulle's message just might have been trapped under the rubble, but nobody seemed to notice, as the film added Oscars for best picture, best direction, and best screenplay.

Like most epic works, *The Bridge On the River Kwai* stimulated a controversy over its historical validity with everyone from scholars to actual P.O.W. laborers attempting to set the record straight. And, like most epic works, the fiction came to supersede the facts.

William Holden was thirty-nine when *Kwai* premiered. Approaching his fortieth birthday, he could have looked back with satisfaction on the recent years that had brought him an Oscar and saw him contribute to several others, kept him rooted among top box-office draws (the top in 1954), and made him independently, irrevocably wealthy—had he been the sort of man to look back. But he was more on the run than ever.

"After so long a time, I think I can say that acting is not a profession for a thinking man. The writer dictates your thoughts, the director tells you where to move, the costume man dresses you. I pick up the check which enables me to try to live a better life on a level other than an actor's."—to the *New York Herald Tribune,* September, 1960

THE HOLDEN GRAIL

The urge for mobility never deserted Holden. As far back as his 1937 cross-country road trip, he had found release and relaxation in travel. By electing to make the bulk of his films abroad, he finally came upon the ideal method and means for stoking the perpetual motion machine known as William Holden.

After *Kwai,* the next stop in his global filmwork was England and Sir Carol Reed's *The Key* (1958). From a Jan de Hartog novel, *Stella,* Carl Foreman distilled a screenplay that relates the unglamorous plight of ocean-going tugboat crews of the British Salvage Service, called upon in the early stages of World War II to rescue disabled ships of the Atlantic convoys from German U-boats.

The Key unfolds a story of a woman named Stella (Sophia Loren) who, after losing her lover to a rescue mission, takes up with his pal, who had been given a key to her flat for her safekeeping and protection. There begins a kinky tradition in which the current holder of the key bequeaths a spare to a chosen heir in the event of death. The plot is a bit murky on this score, but clarifies when tugboat captain Holden inherits the key, falls in love with Stella, and decides to buck the tradition. Romance is then ushered to the wings when Holden is called away on a suicide mission, as the narrative takes on surprisingly Gothic overtones, complete with eerie music. Sure enough, his tug is demolished but miraculously, he survives.

Here is where the film diverges. In the foreign version, Holden resumes life with Stella, but Foreman feared the coupling might run afoul of the U.S. Production Code, so Reed shot a second ending where Holden suffers through but parts with Stella. As it happened, last-minute Code revisions made the auxiliary finish unnecessary, but it was too late to recall the first round of prints. Opening night audiences saw something decidedly different than what went into general release.

THE KEY (1958). With Sophia Loren

For all this, Holden turns in a leathery and versatile depiction of the captain, and is flattered visually by the use of high-contrast black-and-white film stock.

In a very real and vital sense, William Holden had always been a competitive actor, at his best under the pressure of trying to please a fine director or stand his ground opposite a prestigious co-star. *The Horse Soldiers* (1959), co-starring John Wayne and directed by old master John Ford, delivered both incentives plus a handsome third —$750,000 in salary against 20% of the picture's gross.

The story platform was an actual Civil War episode in which a Union Cavalry unit conducted a chancey raid three hundred miles behind enemy lines to attack Newton Station, the key supply depot for Vicksburg. Every bit as daring as the raid was the run back to safety at Union-controlled Baton Rouge. Under less capable direction, it might have been the stuff of which lifeless programmers are made. As Ford's canvas, the narrative assumes an epic scope of both pictorial and human grandeur. William Clothier's classicist camerawork captures Ford's vision, and Holden and Wayne animate it as could no others.

Hips ajar, arms aswing, and voice adrawl, Wayne plays the rough-and-tumble Union Colonel asked to engineer the raid. As the smooth but manly Major Surgeon assigned to the detail, Holden is a plucky and urbane rival for the shambling Wayne. The two set the terms of an ongoing debate between a soldierly singlemindedness and a humanist embracing of the Hippocratic oath over the Army oath. It is a testament to Ford's growth as an artist that he ascribes courage and dignity to both, to the detriment of neither.

The film receives capable acting support from Hoot Gibson, Carleton Young, and black former tennis star Althea Gibson. As for the two stars Holden and Wayne, there was no stolen thunder; each was sublime. Their male and actor's egos emerged invigorated, with Holden earning a high compliment from Wayne: "Someday I'll kill that guy. He makes acting look so easy."

That could be said when Holden was acting, not sleep-walking, as he did in his next two pictures, *The World of Suzie Wong* (1960) and *Satan Never Sleeps* (1962). Playing a portrait artist in the one and a

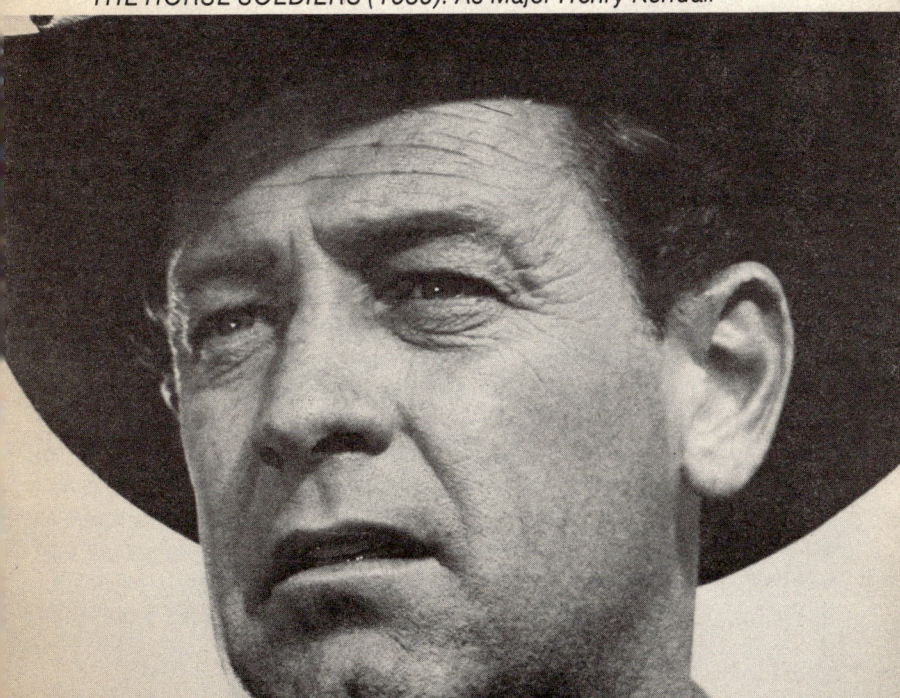

THE HORSE SOLDIERS (1959). As Major Henry Kendall

THE WORLD OF SUZIE WONG (1960). With Nancy Kwan

priest in the other, he was badly miscast in both.

Suzie Wong, for all its bustling location footage, is a prettified travesty on the sordid life of prostitution in Hong Kong, with Holden once more snuggling with a woman of easy virtue, played here by Nancy Kwan. Holden's poor showing might have received harder treatment at the hands of the press had it not been for Miss Kwan's glaringly inept whore-with-a-heart-of-plastic, who frisks about, coquettishly displaying her conspicuous behind in one scene after another.

Holden does little better by chastity in Leo McCarey's directorial swan song, *Satan Never Sleeps.* There is some passably chummy banter between Holden and Clifton Webb as two Catholic priests, but it all seems hopelessly trivial against the disastrously ill-chosen setting of 1949 China. The depth of McCarey's grasp of the late stages of Communist takeover of that country is summed up in Webb's repeated oath, "Those Red rascals!"

Actually, this nostalgic nod to the director's earlier *Going My Way* (1944) might have tread water in a more genial locale. Holden has a certain feel for his character's comically bungling piety, and France Nuyen (who played Suzie Wong on stage) is coy but not cloying as a dreamy peasant girl. Still, McCarey is operating off impulses that are worlds apart: screwball comedy, quaint religious humor, and gut-level anti-Communism. The predictable result is the irrelevant stew of *Satan Never Sleeps*.

Anyone looking for the reason behind Holden's association with such slender fare didn't have to look far. In late 1959, he and his family joined the exodus of top-dollar show people to Europe, and the Holdens moved into a comfortable four-bedroom house overlooking Lake Leman in St. Prex, Switzerland. Tax shelter had been a consideration in the move, but not the deciding factor. Holden, the entrepreneur, had bankrolled flourishing investments in Hong Kong (an import-export business and a broadcasting outfit) and had recently become a founder and charter member of the posh Mt. Kenya Safari Club in East Africa. Switzerland was a likely jumping

SATAN NEVER SLEEPS (1962). With France Nuyen and Clifton Webb

THE COUNTERFEIT TRAITOR (1962). As Eric Erickson

off spot for this budding internationalist, and it offered asylum from the shallow whirl of Hollywood life. In practice, Holden reserved little time for refuge, traveling constantly and logging a staggering yearly average of some 200,000 air miles. Acting was, at best, getting his divided attention.

Friends and admirers mourned the fact that so talented an actor was fast becoming another pinstriped dollar-slave. Holden did not see it that way: "After forty-five motion pictures I have no illusions about myself. I'm not an actor. I've never been one. What I am is a contemporary reporter. Films set in a sound stage no longer hold any glamour for me. They're just a place to work. To be an actor, you have to be one of two things: calloused or talented, and I'm neither."

That said, he went to work on George Seaton's *The Counterfeit Traitor* (1962). And, unless the critics were uniformly wrong, Holden was acting in spite of himself.

Borrowing from the true-life heroism of Eric Erickson, the film tells of an American-born, Swedish-naturalized, apolitical businessman who is pressed into service as a spy during the Second World War by Allied Intelligence agents hoping to tap his contacts within Nazi Germany. As a cover for the operation, Erickson must pose as a Nazi sympathizer. The narrative stitches together a collection of suspenseful cloak and dagger episodes that eventually lead to Erickson's discovery and narrow escape. At its portly 140-minute running length, the film time and again verges on the overblown, but rebounds each time with a potent sequence.

With its exceptional supporting cast of European actors, stylish photography by Jean Bourgoin, and polished direction by Seaton, *The Counterfeit Traitor* succeeds as a gripping, quasi-biography. Although looking a bit tuckered, overweight, and puffy around the eyes, Holden is energetic and engrossing. As narrator and principal actor, he sustains the film through its various strengths and weaknesses.

Elsewhere, Holden and other celebrity expatriates were coming under renewed criticism for the supposed tax drain they had initiated. For its part, the Hollywood press could not bring itself to believe that the one-time model citizen had grown disaffected with life in America. For Holden, the most telling blow came when he learned that scattered locals of studio technician unions were planning to picket *The Counterfeit Traitor,* charging that such foreign-made, American-backed productions were

THE COUNTERFEIT TRAITOR (1962). With Lilli Palmer

taking money out of the pockets of working men at home. The actor's reply did not mince words, "I really couldn't care less about what they say about me in Hollywood. I'm going to live the way I want to live, and nobody's going to tell me how."

The play of events was slowly dampening Holden's interest in acting. In the ensuing six years, he appeared in only six films. And from the looks of those, his actor's judgment was clouding as well.

Eager to plug his beloved Africa, Holden held forth in Jack Cardiff's *The Lion* (1962), a film he should have avoided like the plague. Released for the holiday season, it was ostensibly an adventure-primer on the terrain and culture of the African bush. However, the story gets so sucked into the undertow of psychodramatic crosscurrents that the toothy jungle beasts begin to look tame by comparison. Little Pamela Franklin files an apprentice-like performance as the confused child overly attached to a lion, which is more than can be said of the glacial Capucine, as her mother. Holden is competent as dad, and nothing more. The scenic footage, shot largely in and around Holden's Safari Club, is adequate, but shrivels beside the breathtaking camerawork of Howard Hawks' *Hatari!*, released earlier that year.

If the personally catastrophic *Sabrina* ten years before hadn't

THE LION (1962). With Pamela Franklin

taught William Holden to steer clear of drawing-room comedy and Audrey Hepburn, his next picture would, once and for all. *Paris When it Sizzles* (1964), from a French film *Holiday For Henrietta* (1955), contains lethal doses of each. A shoddy conceit by screenwriter George Axelrod, the story nominally concerns a screenwriter on the spot for a deadline, who, with his hired typist, embarks on flights of fantasy trying to chart a scenario to put under the snappy title, *The Girl Who Stole the Eiffel Tower*. It is half-baked, antic comedy that grinds like an antique.

The hair-dyed, tired-eyed Holden is limber but unattractive in a role that even the ageless Cary Grant would have found unwieldy. Holden's hack writer actually seems to shrink before the harsh interior lighting. In a wardrobe that is De Givenchy-ed to the teeth, Miss Hepburn seems to comprehend that, in lieu of a worthwhile motion picture, the least she can do is be ravishing. There were critics who also thought that was the most she could do.

All the while, the gossip mills were cranking out news of a Holden-Capucine affair, started when they filmed *The Lion*. The stories fanned the actor's already seething bitterness toward the press, but also may have figured in Ardis Holden's request for a legal separation in 1963. For all the in-

PARIS WHEN IT SIZZLES (1964). With Audrey Hepburn

THE SEVENTH DAWN (1964). With Tetsuro Tamba and Susannah York

nuendo, very little was known, except that Capucine was a former Dior and De Givenchy model.

The rest was left to the imagination, and imagination was what it took to make sense of the Holden-Capucine vehicle, *The Seventh Dawn* (1964). Filmed on location in Malaya, the picture is a hodgepodge of surfaces that never quite come together at the cinematic or narrative level. Its topic of post-war struggles between native Communists and British Colonialists in Indochina has too many snags to propel the final race against the clock of the film's title.

Wisely out of doors and away from the Klieg lights, Holden looks tanned and fit. The puffiness is gone from his face and the hint of paunch from his girth. As the vigorous, shrewd and politically neutral plantation owner, he seems comfortably in his element and the enthusiasm shows in his acting. Yet the story is so implausible and labyrinthine that the effort is wasted.

In some hard-sell casting,

ALVAREZ KELLY (1966). With Richard Widmark and Richard Rust

Capucine plays Holden's Eurasian mistress. Their relationship is constructed smartly and adultly, devoid of twitting apologetics, and audiences hoping for feverish romance saw, instead, a mature and loving couple. Beyond this, however, Capucine's character is left little to do. Mostly, she awaits execution on the seventh dawn after a kangaroo court conviction, and looks exotically lovely in her prison cell in a half-lit, Nefertiti-like profile.

The overriding question was, "When would Bill Holden get back on his feet and act in a creditable film?" *The Seventh Dawn* obviously was not the answer.

Nor, for that matter, was *Alvarez Kelly* (1966), another Civil War rehash for which the actor made a rare stateside visit in late 1965. The real fireworks preceded the film by months. Holden had been content to spar with the press, jabbing and ducking whenever he felt himself being crowded. When the saintly *New York Times* requested an interview, he decided to square off, and let loose with a manifesto that landed like a haymaker to the jaw. In truth, he was posing all the right questions, scalding as they were.

> Why should I tell anyone what I think about anything? Just because I am a star and supposedly have an image to uphold, why does that mean I

should pat orphans on the head or play benefits every night or give my opinions to reporters? I don't give a damn about my image. My obligation to the public is performance—what they see on the screen. That's all the public should ask of me. Anyway, that's all I'm giving.

The trouble was, he wasn't giving too well. In the title role of Edward Dmytryk's *Alvarez Kelly,* his face again looked furrowed and splotchy, and his expression hangdog. He had been drawn by a character that he found curiously savory, a dapper war profiteer selling cattle to the highest bidder. But Alvarez Kelly the character holds up better than *Alvarez Kelly* the motion picture. Dmytryk's ordinarily stout direction is gaunt, perhaps stumped over how to make a handful of cows look like the 2500 steers called for in the script. The script, in its turn, fritters away too much time on leaden dialogue, and not enough on imaginative plotting.

The film's greatest single hurdle is Richard Widmark's patch-eyed Rebel Colonel, who hijacks Kelly and his beef. He is broody and brutish, with a cornpone accent that sounds as if it's never been south of Minneapolis. The embattled

CASINO ROYALE (1967). With John Huston, Charles Boyer, David Niven, and Kurt Kasznar

THE DEVIL'S BRIGADE (1968). With Andrew Prine

alliance that evolves between the Colonel and Kelly cries for the muscular grace of the truce between Wayne and Holden in *The Horse Soldiers*.

Producer Sol C. Siegel was acutely aware of the picture's many flaws. Upon completion, he sent it straight to the neighborhood theaters and hoped for the best, which was none too good.

As if paced by some sprung inner mechanism, Holden's hobbling filmwork accelerated his off-screen life. He drank hard, lived fast, and pushed himself to dizzying speeds. On July 26, 1966, it all came telescoping in an instant. Outside of Lucca, Italy, on the road from Florence to Pisa, Holden was driving a sports car, accompanied by two friends from New York City, Sarah and Susan West. He prepared to pass a slow-moving vehicle and angled out, but the driver failed to allow room and before Holden could return to his lane, he collided with another motorist traveling from the opposite direction. The Holden party was shaken but unhurt. The lone occupant of the other car, an Italian businessman named Giorgio Novelli, was dead.

That October, Holden was convicted of manslaughter and given an eight-month sentence, suspended due to the extenuating circumstances. He was not present at the sentencing, but later paid $80,000 to Novelli's wife, Carla, in an out-of-court settlement. Less than a month after the trial, Holden's father died of a respiratory ailment, in Palm Springs, California.

The dual tragedies had a numbing effect. Except for an almost catatonic cameo in Charles K. Feldman's spy-spoofing extravaganza, *Casino Royale* (1967), Holden withdrew from public life. Given serious pause, he began reordering his personal life, and started by attempting a reconciliation with Ardis.

William Holden did not appear in another motion picture until the spring of 1968, when he starred in Andrew McLaglen's *The Devil's Brigade*. The film centers on the 1942 formation of the First Special Service Corps, comprised of highly-trained Canadian commandos and, as the scenarist would have us believe, a generous sprinkling of psychopathic GI riff-raff.

The Devil's Brigade came under fierce criticism as a weak sister to *The Dirty Dozen,* which opened just a few months prior and exploited a similar premise. What the critics failed to note was that McLaglen was working in the brawling, regimental vein of his mentor, John Ford (who had guided his father, Victor McLaglen to a 1935 Oscar in *The Informer*). In that light, the film is a somewhat

THE WILD BUNCH (1969). As Pike Bishop

THE WILD BUNCH (1969). With Ben Johnson, Warren Oates, and Ernest Borgnine

stylized, peripherally naturalistic comment on the deadly business of war, where comradeship and duty mean more than fame and glory.

Neither showy nor verbally flamboyant, Holden presents the Corps' senior officer as calculating and methodical, personable and professional, if a bit stiff-limbed. It is the very performance director McLaglen wanted.

The critical drubbing of the film notwithstanding, Holden's acting was regaining momentum. He had no idea how quickly it would snowball.

By 1969, filmmakers had come to believe that just about everything of gravity that could be said about the classic American West had already been said. For some directors, that meant either imitation or abandonment. For Sam Peckinpah, that meant one last definitive epitaph to the Western.

The result was *The Wild Bunch* (1969), a film which fostered extravagant arguments both pro and con, and which was, for better or worse, a landmark motion picture. Seizing the vanishing frontier as its backdrop, the story opens in 1913 and traces the sinking fortunes of old-style outlawry, as epitomized by the arthritic bank-robber, Pike Bishop. Once a member of the notorious Wild Bunch, Bishop now rides with a dissolute band of thugs. Their plan to plunder a bank in a Texas bordertown backfires as they are caught in a gory ambush, laid by Deke Thornton, himself a former member of the Bunch who has been blackmailed into bounty hunting.

Bishop and gang flee to Mexico as nemesis Thornton gives chase. For want of gainful marauding, the outlaws throw in with a cut-throat Mexican Federal General willing to pay for weapons. The gang completes its side of the bargain, but out of equal parts sport and spite, the General detains one of Bishop's men for torture. The gang's sense of loyalty and professionalism erupts in indignation, as they challenge the Federal soldiers and, though overwhelmingly outmanned, they gain the upper hand in the bloodletting before being brought down to the man.

Every bit as meaningful as the story is the telling. Peckinpah's master design here is a graphic iconoclasm of images, which is to say that his victims bleed, often profusely and vividly, thus stripping the romantic notions of Western gunplay to its naked truth. With no compromise for his audience, Peckinpah arrives at his bleak epitaph.

The expert camerawork of Lucien Ballard is inestimable in coloring the film's varied visual moods, and is edited to perfection by Peckinpah and Louis Lombardo, who construct an electrifying opening montage of flash cuts and in-

THE CHRISTMAS TREE (1969). With Brook Fuller and Virna Lisi

WILD ROVERS (1971). With Ryan O'Neal

terrupted slow-motion.

With all the technical brilliance, it is easy to overlook the acting, a grave error, especially since William Holden gives the finest performance of his late career. Physically sturdy though slightly pinch-shouldered, and speaking in a voice that is gravelly, at times husky, his Pike Bishop looks and sounds like a bandit confronting his twilight years. In his craggy, bewhiskered face, we see the disquieting glint of a killer, alongside the disarming glance of a loner. Holden's textured portrait encompasses the key conflicts of *The Wild Bunch*, operating like a fine, precise wheel in the film's larger mechanism.

What first appeared to be a career renaissance turned out to be more of a downslope. As something of a sop to those offended by the violence of *The Wild Bunch*, Holden returned later that year in *The Christmas Tree* (1969), a teary contrivance about a young boy who suffers lethal radiation poisoning. The film lacks conviction at all levels as commentary on the nuclear age, leaving the boy's Yuletide demise essentially pointless. As the loving father, Holden is mechanical and drab, but then, director Terence Young's admitted criterion for the role had been an actor whose face would not stand out in a crowd. Coincidentally, there were no crowds in the pic-

THE REVENGERS (1972).
As John Benedict

BREEZY (1973). With Kay Lenz

ture, or outside the theaters where it played.

Heeding his better instincts, Holden was soon back in the saddle, only it was not a particularly choice saddle. *Wild Rovers* (1971), produced, written, and directed by Blake Edwards, is witness to the fact that a Western made without a unifying overview is just so much piecemeal, dime-novel fodder.

Hoping to latch on to the coattails of *The Wild Bunch, Wild Rovers,* (far from being about wandering dogs), depicts a pair of drovers who tire of the monotony of cattle herding and undertake an ill-planned bank robbery intended to bring them to that elusive cowboy utopia, a ranch in Mexico. The heist ticks off smoothly but the escape southward is botched and the two are eventually killed by a posse.

Edwards was too steeped in frothy comedy to cope with this story. But if his head is not exactly in the right place, his heart is, and, disconnected as they are, there are some effectively lyrical moments. What lifts the film from discontinuity and cradles the lyricism is Holden's presence as the aging drover. Wearing a brush mustache as he did in *The Wild Bunch,* he is weathered and wizened, yet a droll folk philosopher who may ache in the joints, but is still active in the beer joints and brothels. Ryan O'Neal, his puppy-like sidekick, is something of a companion idolator and advertisement for Holden's character, devised by Edwards as a short-cut to myth.

Holden does not bend under the strain of carrying the picture. In fact, it acts as a tonic—his confidence feeds an aura, and that aura is his ticket to the role. Holden plays with a simple honesty that even endows the film's downbeat

OPEN SEASON (1974). With Mike Sambeck

ending with a certain poignant beauty, as he rides toward death through Monument Valley, poking along and crowing the drover's song in a voice like cactus.

Squeezing the last bit of mileage out of Holden's *Wild Bunch* mystique, Daniel Mann enlisted the actor in *The Revengers* (1972), a formula Western concerning a rancher's search for the man who massacred his family. The picture is secondhand material, but is does permit Holden a pair of reunions, first with Susan Hayward, his friend from *Young and Willing* thirty years before, here playing a gentle frontier nurse, and second, with his son Scott, playing a bit part as a cavalry lieutenant.

Drastically changing pace, Holden swapped his Stetson for Brooks Brothers, and appeared in the contemporary May-December romance, *Breezy* (1973), directed by Clint Eastwood, himself a graduate cum laude of the tumbleweed. Holden plays a fifty-year-old businessman divorcé, whose workaday solitude is shaken by a curvaceous seventeen-year-old flower child, Breezy (Kay Lenz). An improbable romance blossoms, and, despite a host of obstacles, the two decide to remain together so long as their love lasts. Given the material, the performances are sensitive, and Holden's son Scott elbows in again, briefly, as a veterinarian.

Well-meaning as it is, *Breezy* was already passé before it came out, hip generation critiques having been demoted to the past culture of the sixties. Were such preachy romance possible, Eastwood and Holden still would not have been the men for the job.

After the puncturing letdown of *Breezy,* William Holden appeared in a small role in *Open Season* (1974), a grim drama concerning three sadistic war veterans who indulge in a yearly ritual of kidnapping, abusing, then releasing and hunting down a hapless random couple. Holden played a man bent on revenging the death of his daughter, who was raped by the three veterans.

Later that year, he resurfaced in the Irwin Allen disaster spectacle, *The Towering Inferno* (1974). Wrinkled but robust, his grey-templed, seasoned grace leads to one of the notable performances in a cast roster that reads like a latter-day box office hall of fame. As the builder of the world's tallest skyscraper (which turns out to be the world's tallest tinder box), Holden gives a performance precisely contoured to the character—sympathetically executive. His standout contribution is no small accomplishment opposite the current top draws in the industry, and a script that literally places him between hell and high water.

With this performance, the verdict was in. William Holden was not about to go to seed. Not by a long shot.*

*As of this writing, he is scheduled to appear in an important role in Paddy Chayefsky's *Network*, a satirical comedy-drama about the inner workings of television. His co-stars are Faye Dunaway and Peter Finch.

THE TOWERING INFERNO (1974). With Richard Chamberlain

"My life seems to change every ten years. There was Hollywood, then ten years in the Far East, then Africa. Now I wonder what comes next."—to *The New York Times*, July, 1971

FULL CIRCLE

From the time William Holden first won notice in *Golden Boy*, the visible actor had never been the full measure of the man. He was a sprinter, and the press, friends, and even his own self-awareness often lagged in the wake of his fame. But the months spent in retreat in Kenya over the past decade had done much to stay his stride.

Although Holden's marriage to Ardis finally dissolved in July of 1971, his infatuation with fast cars and faster women had run its course. His abiding passion was an austere 1260-acre game ranch, adjacent to the Mt. Kenya Safari Club, where he educated himself as a conservationist, meticulously studying the area's unique flora and fauna. Hoping to gain exposure for the vista, he persuaded producer David Wolper to shoot a television documentary in the vicinity, *William Holden's Untamed World* (1969).

Holden himself soon became the target of some friendly persuasion, and was ultimately coaxed into his first television dramatic role, appearing as Joe "Bumper" Morgan in a special two-hour treatment of the Joseph Wambaugh novel, *The Blue Knight* (1973), about a dedicated Los Angeles beat cop. Holden's absorbing characterization earned him an Emmy Award, and an invitation to continue the role in a series. But he was still too much in motion to settle into routine, and was busily promoting other ventures, including yet another conservation project (a wild-life sanctuary for birds and primates in the Bismarck Archipelago of New Guinea).

By the spring of 1976, The William Holden Odyssey had come full circle back to Southern California, though he was hardly one to simply find storybook happiness in his old Pasadena backyard.

Carefully weighing the global options, Holden selected the Coachella Valley, on the outskirts of Palm Springs, where he designed a house and supervised its construction. As a gesture of truce, he set about transplanting varieties of exotic African vegetation on the Valley floor, while making the residence a home, and something more. "It will be a kind of workshop for me. There are a lot of

THE BLUE KNIGHT (1973). With Lee Remick

things I want to do, a lot of thoughts I haven't had." And Palm Springs social life was nowhere in the picture, "I just can't waste the time socializing when I can be alone, informing myself with a good book."

William Holden had come home to himself. And Hollywood would get a second chance to learn that its estranged protégé was not a tarnished Golden Boy, but a worldly, greying man, with years of incisive acting well within reach.

Beyond that possibility, the final footnote is Holden's, alone.

BIBLIOGRAPHY

Bart, Peter, "Holden: All-American Boy?" *The New York Times*, December 12, 1965.
Franchey, John R., "That's Holden For You," *Photoplay*, July 1940.
Gehman, Richard, "Still The Golden Boy," *McCall's*, July, 1962.
Harmetz, Aljean, "Don't Get Personal With Bill Holden," *The New York Times*, July 4, 1971.
Holland, Jack, "Is The Press Fair to Actors?" *Silver Screen*, July, 1951.
Hyams, Joe, "Hollywood's Busiest Leading Man," *Cue*, April 24, 1954.
Hyams, Joe, " 'The Wasted Life' of William Holden," *New York Herald Tribune*, September 28, 1960.
Lundy, Dori, "William Holden: The Man," *Palm Springs Life*, November, 1975.
Madsen, Axel, *Billy Wilder*, Bloomington: Indiana University Press, 1969.
Marill, Alvin H., "William Holden, Doubted His Acting Ability But Not His Business Know-How," *Films in Review*, October, 1973.
Martin, Pete, "Hollywood's Most Improbable Star," *Saturday Evening Post*, August 28, September 4, 1954.
The New Yorker, "Profiles, The Player," October 21, 1961.
Nugent, F. S., "Golden Holden," *Colliers*, June 2, 1951.
Phillips, Dee, "Average Score: Terrific," *Photoplay*, April, 1955.
Plummer, Charlotte and Denis, "Extraordinary Ordinary Guy," *The New York Times Magazine*, January 19, 1958.
Proctor, Kay, "Lady Luck's Protégé," *Screen Book*, July, 1939.
Quirk, Lawrence J., *The Films of William Holden*, Secaucus: The Citadel Press, 1973.
Reid, James, "Gilding 'Golden Boy'," *Silver Screen*, October, 1939.
Scott, Vernon, "Right Roles Vital," *U.P.I.*, January 22, 1953.
Swanson, Pauline, "Mr. Dynamite," *Photoplay*, January, 1952.
Time, "The Conquest of Smiling Jim," February 27, 1956.
Time, "On Location, Film Rites in Kenya," September 13, 1968.

THE FILMS OF WILLIAM HOLDEN

The director's name follows the release date. A (c) following the release date indicates that the film is in color. Sp indicates screenplay and b/o indicates based on.

1. GOLDEN BOY. Columbia, 1939. *Rouben Mamoulian*. Sp: Lewis Meltzer, Daniel Taradash, Sarah Y. Mason, and Victor Heerman, b/o play by Clifford Odets. Cast: Barbara Stanwyck, Adolphe Menjou, Lee J. Cobb, Joseph Calleia, Sam Levene, Edward S. Brophy, Beatrice Blinn, William H. Strauss.

2. INVISIBLE STRIPES. Warners, 1940. *Lloyd Bacon*. Sp: Warren Duff, b/o original story by Jonathan Finn and book by Warden Lewis E. Lawes. Cast: George Raft, Jane Bryan, Humphrey Bogart, Flora Robson, Paul Kelly, Lee Patrick, Henry O'Neill, Frankie Thomas.

3. OUR TOWN. United Artists, 1940. *Sam Wood*. Sp: Thornton Wilder, Frank Craven, and Harry Chandlee, b/o play by Thornton Wilder. Cast: Frank Craven, Martha Scott, Fay Bainter, Beulah Bondi, Thomas Mitchell, Guy Kibbee, Stuart Erwin, Phillip Wood, Doro Merande.

4. THOSE WERE THE DAYS. Paramount, 1940. *J. Theodore Reed*. Sp: Don Hartman, b/o the "Siwash" Stories by George Fitch. Cast: Bonita Granville, Ezra Stone, Judith Barrett, Vaughan Glaser, Lucien Littlefield, Richard Denning, Tom Rutherford, Phillip Terry.

5. ARIZONA. Columbia, 1941. *Wesley Ruggles*. Sp: Claude Binyon, b/o story by Clarence Budington Kelland. Cast: Jean Arthur, Warren William, Porter Hall, Paul Harvey, George Chandler, Byron Foulger, Regis Toomey, Paul Lopez.

6. I WANTED WINGS. Paramount, 1941. *Mitchell Leisen*. Sp: Richard Maibaum, Lieut. Beirne Lay Jr., and Sig Herzig, b/o story by Eleanore Griffin and Frank Wead and book *I Wanted Wings* by Lt. Beirne Lay Jr. Cast: Ray Milland, Wayne Morris, Brian Donlevy, Constance Moore, Veronica Lake, Harry Davenport, Phil Brown, Edward Fielding.

7. TEXAS. Columbia, 1941. *George Marshall*. Sp: Horace McCoy, Lewis Meltzer, and Michael Blankfort, b/o story by Lewis Meltzer and Michael Blankfort. Cast: Glenn Ford, Claire Trevor, George Bancroft, Edgar Buchanan, Don Beddoe, Andrew Tombes, Addison Richards, Edmund MacDonald.

8. THE REMARKABLE ANDREW. Paramount, 1942. *Stuart Heisler*. Sp: Dalton Trumbo, b/o novel by Dalton Trumbo. Cast: Ellen Drew, Brian Donlevy,

Rod Cameron, Richard Webb, Porter Hall, Frances Gifford, Nydia Westman, Montagu Love.

9. THE FLEET'S IN. Paramount, 1942. *Victor Schertzinger.* Sp: Walter De Leon, Sid Silvers and Ralph Spence, b/o story by Monte Brice and J. Walter Ruben and play by Kenyon Nicholson and Charles Robinson. Cast: Dorothy Lamour, Eddie Bracken, Betty Hutton, Cass Daley, Gil Lamb, Leif Erickson, Betty Jane Rhodes, Lorraine and Ragnan, Jimmy Dorsey and his Band. Previously filmed in 1936 as *Lady, Be Careful* and remade in 1952 as *Sailor Beware.*

10. MEET THE STEWARTS. Columbia, 1942. *Alfred E. Green.* Sp: Karen De Wolf, b/o Elizabeth Dunn's Candy and Mike Stewart magazine stories. Cast: Frances Dee, Grant Mitchell, Marjorie Gateson, Anne Revere, Roger Clark, Danny Mummert, Ann Gillis, Margaret Hamilton.

11. YOUNG AND WILLING. United Artists-Cinema Guild, 1943. *Edward H. Griffith.* Sp: Virginia Van Upp, b/o play *Out of the Frying Pan* by Francis Swann. Cast: Eddie Bracken, Robert Benchley, Susan Hayward, Martha O'Driscoll, Barbara Britton, James Brown, Florence MacMichael, Mabel Paige.

12. BLAZE OF NOON. Paramount, 1947. *John Farrow.* Sp: Frank Wead and Arthur Sheekman, b/o novel by Ernest K. Gann. Cast: Anne Baxter, William Bendix, Sonny Tufts, Sterling Hayden, Howard da Silva, Johnny Sands, Jean Wallace, Edith King.

13. DEAR RUTH. Paramount, 1947. *William D. Russell.* Sp: Arthur Sheekman, b/o play by Norman Krasna. Cast: Joan Caulfield, Edward Arnold, Mary Philips, Mona Freeman, Billy De Wolfe, Virginia Welles, Kenny O'Morrison, Irving Bacon.

14. VARIETY GIRL. Paramount, 1947. *George Marshall.* Sp: Edmund Hartman, Frank Tashlin, Robert Welch, and Monte Brice. Cast: Mary Hatcher, Olga San Juan, De Forest Kelley, William Demarest, Frank Faylen, with guest stars.

15. RACHEL AND THE STRANGER. RKO Radio, 1948. *Norman Foster.* Sp: Waldo Salt, b/o story by Howard Fast. Cast: Loretta Young, Robert Mitchum, Gary Gray, Tom Tully, Sara Haden, Frank Ferguson, Walter Baldwin, Regina Wallace.

16. APARTMENT FOR PEGGY. Twentieth Century-Fox, 1948 (c). *George Seaton.* Sp: George Seaton, b/o story by Faith Baldwin. Cast: Jeanne Crain, Edmund Gwenn, Gene Lockhart, Griff Barnett, Randy Stuart, Marion Marshall, Pati Behrs, Henri Letondal.

17. THE DARK PAST. Columbia, 1948. *Rudolph Mate.* Sp: Philip MacDonald, Michael Blankfort, and Albert Duffy, adap. by Malvin Wald and Oscar Saul, b/o play *Blind Alley* by James Warwick. Cast: Nina Foch, Lee J. Cobb, Adele Jergens, Stephen Dunne, Lois Maxwell, Berry Kroeger, Steven Geray, Wilton Graff. Previously filmed in 1939 as *Blind Alley.*

18. THE MAN FROM COLORADO. Columbia, 1949 (c). *Henry Levin.* Sp: Robert D. Andrews and Ben Maddow, b/o story by Borden Chase. Cast: Glenn Ford, Ellen Drew, Ray Collins, Edgar Buchanan, Jerome Courtland, James Millican, Jim Bannon, William "Bill" Phillips.

19. STREETS OF LAREDO. Paramount, 1949 (c). *Leslie Fenton.* Sp: Charles Marquis Warren, b/o story by Louis Stevens and Elizabeth Hill. Cast: William Bendix, Macdonald Carey, Mona Freeman, Stanley Ridges, Alfonso Bedoya, Ray Teal, Clem Bevans, James Bell.

20. MISS GRANT TAKES RICHMOND. Columbia, 1949. *Lloyd Bacon.* Sp: Nat Perrin, Devery Freeman, Frank Tashlin, b/o story by Devery Freeman. Cast: Lucille Ball, Janis Carter, James Gleason, Gloria Henry, Frank McHugh, George Cleveland, Stephen Dunne, Arthur Space.

21. DEAR WIFE. Paramount, 1950. *Richard Haydn.* Sp: Arthur Sheekman and N. Richard Nash, written as a sequel to Norman Krasna's *Dear Ruth.* Cast: Joan Caulfield, Billy De Wolfe, Mona Freeman, Edward Arnold, Arleen Whelan, Mary Philips, Harry Von Zell, Raymond Roe.

22. FATHER IS A BACHELOR. Columbia, 1950. *Norman Foster.* Sp: Aleen Leslie and James Edward Grant, b/o story by James Edward Grant. Cast: Coleen Gray, Mary Jane Saunders, Charles Winninger, Stuart Erwin, Clinton Sundberg, Gary Gray, Sig Ruman, Billy Gray.

23. SUNSET BOULEVARD. Paramount, 1950. *Billy Wilder.* Sp: Charles Brackett, Billy Wilder, and D.M. Marshman, Jr., b/o story "A Can of Beans" by Charles Brackett and Billy Wilder. Cast: Gloria Swanson, Erich von Stroheim, Nancy Olson, Fred Clark, Lloyd Gough, Jack Webb, Franklyn Farnum, Larry Blake.

24. UNION STATION. Paramount, 1950. *Rudolph Maté.* Sp: Sydney Boehm, b/o story by Thomas Walsh. Cast: Nancy Olson, Barry Fitzgerald, Lyle Bettger, Jan Sterling, Allene Roberts, Herbert Heyes, Don Dunning, Fred Graff.

25. BORN YESTERDAY. Columbia, 1950. *George Cukor.* Sp: Albert Mannheimer, b/o play by Garson Kanin. Cast: Broderick Crawford, Judy Holliday, Howard St. John, Frank Otto, Larry Oliver, Barbara Brown, Grandon Rhodes, Claire Carleton.

26. FORCE OF ARMS. Warners, 1951. *Michael Curtiz*. Sp: Orin Jannings, b/o story by Richard Tregaskis. Cast: Nancy Olson, Frank Lovejoy, Gene Evans, Dick Wesson, Paul Picerni, Katherine Warren, Ross Ford, Slats Taylor.

27. SUBMARINE COMMAND. Paramount, 1952. *John Farrow*. Sp: Jonathan Latimer, b/o story by Jonathan Latimer. Cast: Nancy Olson, William Bendix, Don Taylor, Arthur Franz, Darryl Hickman, Peggy Webber, Moroni Olsen, Jack Gregson.

28. BOOTS MALONE. Columbia, 1952. *William Dieterle*. Sp: Milton Holmes. Cast: Johnny Stewart, Stanley Clements, Basil Ruysdael, Carl Benton Reid, Ralph Dumke, Ed Begley, Hugh Sanders, Henry Morgan, Anna Lee.

29. THE TURNING POINT. Paramount, 1952. *William Dieterle*. Sp: Warren Duff, b/o story by Horace McCoy. Cast: Edmond O'Brien, Alexis Smith, Tom Tully, Ed Begley, Don Dayton, Adele Longmire, Ray Teal, Ted De Corsia.

30. STALAG 17. Paramount, 1953. *Billy Wilder*. Sp: Billy Wilder and Edwin Blum b/o play by Donald Bevan and Edmund Trzcinski. Cast: Don Taylor, Otto Preminger, Robert Strauss, Harvey Lembeck, Richard Erdman, Peter Graves, Neville Brand, Sig Ruman, Michael Moore, William Pierson.

31. THE MOON IS BLUE. United Artists, 1953. *Otto Preminger*. Sp: F. Hugh Herbert, b/o his play. Cast: David Niven, Maggie McNamara, Tom Tully, Dawn Addams, Fortunio Bonanova.

32. FOREVER FEMALE. Paramount, 1954. *Irving Rapper*. Sp: Julius J. and Philip G. Epstein, b/o play *Rosalind* by James M. Barrie. Cast: Ginger Rogers, Paul Douglas, Pat Crowley, James Gleason, Jesse White, Marjorie Rambeau, George Reeves, King Donovan, Vic Perrin.

33. ESCAPE FROM FORT BRAVO. MGM, 1954 (c). *John Sturges*. Sp: Frank Fenton, b/o his story by Philip Rock and Michael Pate. Cast: Eleanor Parker, John Forsythe, William Demarest, William Campbell, John Lupton, Richard Anderson, Polly Bergen, Carl Benton Reid.

34. EXECUTIVE SUITE. MGM, 1954. *Robert Wise*. Sp: Ernest Lehman, b/o novel by Cameron Hawley. Cast: Fredric March, Barbara Stanwyck, June Allyson, Walter Pidgeon, Shelley Winters, Paul Douglas, Louis Calhern, Dean Jagger, Nina Foch.

35. SABRINA. Paramount, 1954. *Billy Wilder*. Sp: Billy Wilder, Samuel Taylor, and Ernest Lehman, b/o play *Sabrina Fair* by Samuel Taylor. Cast: Humphrey Bogart, Audrey Hepburn, Walter Hampden, John Williams, Martha Hyer, Joan Vohs, Marcel Hillaire, Nella Walker.

36. THE COUNTRY GIRL. Paramount, 1954. *George Seaton*. Sp: George Seaton, b/o play by Clifford Odets. Cast: Bing Crosby, Grace Kelly, Anthony Ross, Gene Reynolds, Jacqueline Fontaine, Eddie Ryder, Robert Kent, John W. Reynolds.

37. THE BRIDGES AT TOKO-RI. Paramount, 1955 (c). *Mark Robson*. Sp: Valentine Davies, b/o novel by James A. Michener. Cast: Fredric March, Grace Kelly, Mickey Rooney, Robert Strauss, Charles McGraw, Keiko Awaji, Earl Holliman, Richard Shannon.

38. LOVE IS A MANY-SPLENDORED THING. Twentieth Century-Fox, 1955 (c). *Henry King*. Sp: John Patrick, b/o novel by Han Suyin. Cast: Jennifer Jones, Torin Thatcher, Isobel Elsom, Murray Matheson, Virginia Gregg, Richard Loo, Soo Yong, Philip Ahn.

39. PICNIC. Columbia, 1956 (c). *Joshua Logan*. Sp: Daniel Taradash, b/o play by William Inge. Cast: Rosalind Russell, Kim Novak, Betty Field, Susan Strasberg, Cliff Robertson, Arthur O'Connell, Verna Felton, Reta Shaw.

40. THE PROUD AND THE PROFANE. Paramount, 1956. *George Seaton*. Sp: George Seaton, b/o novel by Lucy Herndon Crockett. Cast: Deborah Kerr, Thelma Ritter, Dewey Martin, William Redfield, Ross Bagdasarian, Adam Williams, Marion Ross, Theodore Newton.

41. TOWARD THE UNKNOWN. Warners, 1956 (c). *Mervyn LeRoy*. Sp: Beirne Lay, Jr. Cast: Lloyd Nolan, Virginia Leith, Charles McGraw, Murray Hamilton, Paul Fix, James Garner, L.Q. Jones, Karen Steele.

42. THE BRIDGE ON THE RIVER KWAI. Columbia, 1957 (c). *David Lean*. Sp: Pierre Boulle, b/o novel by Pierre Boulle. Cast: Alec Guinness, Jack Hawkins, Sessue Hayakawa, James Donald, Geoffrey Horne, Andre Morell, Peter Williams, John Boxer.

43. THE KEY. Columbia, 1958. *Carol Reed*. Sp: Carl Foreman, b/o novel *Stella* by Jan de Hartog. Cast: Sophia Loren, Trevor Howard, Oscar Homolka, Kieron Moore, Bernard Lee, Beatrix Lehmann, Noel Purcell, Bryan Forbes.

44. THE HORSE SOLDIERS. United Artists, 1959 (c). *John Ford*. Sp: John Lee Mahin and Martin Rackin, b/o novel by Harold Sinclair. Cast: John Wayne, Constance Towers, Althea Gibson, Hoot Gibson, Anna Lee, Russell Simpson, Stan Jones, Carleton Young.

45. THE WORLD OF SUZIE WONG. Paramount, 1960 (c). *Richard Quine*. Sp: John Patrick, b/o novel by Richard Mason and play by Paul Osborn. Cast:

Nancy Kwan, Sylvia Syms, Michael Wilding, Laurence Naismith, Jacqueline Chan, Andy Ho, Bernard Cribbins, Yvonne Shima.

46. SATAN NEVER SLEEPS. Twentieth Century-Fox, 1962 (c). *Leo McCarey*. Sp: Claude Binyon and Leo McCarey, b/o novel *The China Story* by Pearl S. Buck. Cast: Clifton Webb, France Nuyen, Athene Seyler, Martin Benson, Edith Sharpe, Robert Lee, Weaver Lee, Marie Yong.

47. THE COUNTERFEIT TRAITOR. Paramount, 1962 (c). *George Seaton*. Sp: George Seaton, b/o book by Alexander Klein. Cast: Lilli Palmer, Hugh Griffith, Ernst Schroder, Eva Dahlbeck, Ulf Palme, Carl Raddatz, Helo Gutschwager, Erica Beer.

48. THE LION. Twentieth Century-Fox, 1962 (c). *Jack Cardiff*. Sp: Irene Kamp and Louis Kamp, b/o novel by Joseph Kessel. Cast: Trevor Howard, Capucine, Pamela Franklin, Makara Kwaiha Ramadhani, Zakee, Paul Oduor, Samuel Obiero, Romboh.

49. PARIS WHEN IT SIZZLES. Paramount, 1964 (c). *Richard Quine*. Sp: George Axelrod, b/o story by Julien Duvivier and Henri Jeanson. Cast: Audrey Hepburn, Gregoire Aslan, Noel Coward, Raymonde Bussieres, Christian Duvallex.

50. THE SEVENTH DAWN. United Artists, 1964 (c). *Lewis Gilbert*. Sp: Karl Tunberg, b/o novel *The Durian Tree* by Michael Keon. Cast: Susannah York, Capucine, Tetsuro Tamba, Michael Goodliffe, Allen Cuthbertson, Maurice Denham, Sidney Tafler, Beulah Quo.

51. ALVAREZ KELLY. Columbia, 1966 (c). *Edward Dmytryk*. Sp: Franklin Coen and Elliott Arnold, b/o story by Franklin Coen. Cast: Richard Widmark, Janice Rule, Patrick O'Neal, Victoria Shaw, Roger C. Carmel, Richard Rust, Arthur Franz, Donald Barry.

52. CASINO ROYALE. Columbia, 1967 (c). *John Huston, Kenneth Hughes, Val Guest, Robert Parrish, Joseph McGrath*. Sp: Wolf Mankowitz, John Law, Michael Sayers, b/o novel by Ian Fleming. Cast: Peter Sellers, Ursula Andress, David Niven, Orson Welles, Joanna Pettet, Daliah Lavi, Woody Allen, Charles Boyer.

53. THE DEVIL'S BRIGADE. United Artists, 1968 (c). *Andrew L. McLaglen*. Sp: William Roberts, b/o book by Robert H. Anderson and Colonel George Walton. Cast: Cliff Robertson, Vince Edwards, Michael Rennie, Dana Andrews, Gretchen Wyler, Andrew Prine, Claude Akins, Carroll O'Connor.

54. THE WILD BUNCH. Warners-7 Arts, 1969 (c). *Sam Peckinpah*. Sp: Walon Green and Sam Peckinpah, b/o story by Walon Green and Roy N. Sickner. Cast: Ernest Borgnine, Robert Ryan, Edmond O'Brien, Warren Oates, Jaime Sanchez, Ben Johnson, Emilio Fernandez, Strother Martin.

55. THE CHRISTMAS TREE. Walter Reade-Continental, 1969 (c). *Terence Young*. Sp: Terence Young, b/o novel *L'Arbre de Noel* by Michel Bataille. Cast: Virna Lisi, Andre Bourvil, Brook Fuller, Madeleine Damien, Friedrich Ledebur, Mario Feliciani.

56. WILD ROVERS. MGM, 1971 (c). *Blake Edwards*. Sp: Blake Edwards. Cast: Ryan O'Neal, Karl Malden, Lynn Carlin, Tom Skerritt, Joe Don Baker, James Olson, Leora Dana, Moses Gunn.

57. THE REVENGERS. National General Pictures, 1972 (c). *Daniel Mann*. Sp: Wendell Mayes, b/o story by Steven W. Carabatsos. Cast: Susan Hayward, Ernest Borgnine, Woody Strode, Roger Hanin, Rene Koldehoff, Jorge Luke, Jorge Martinez De Hoyos, Arthur Hunnicutt.

58. BREEZY. Universal, 1973 (c). *Clint Eastwood*. Sp: Jo Heims. Cast: Kay Lenz, Dennis Olivieri, Marj Dusay, Eugene Peterson, Joan Hotchkiss, Roger C. Carmel, Shelley Morrison, Jamie Smith Jackson.

59. OPEN SEASON. Columbia, 1974 (c). *Peter Collinson*. Sp: David Osborn and Liz Charles-Williams. Cast: Peter Fonda, Cornelia Sharpe, John Philip Law, Richard Lynch, Alberto Mendoza.

60. THE TOWERING INFERNO. Twentieth Century-Fox-Warner Brothers, 1974 (c). *John Guillermin and Irwin Allen*. Sp: Stirling Silliphant, b/o novels *The Tower* by Richard Martin Stern and *The Glass Inferno* by Thomas N. Scortia and Frank M. Robinson. Cast: Steve McQueen, Paul Newman, Faye Dunaway, Fred Astaire, Susan Blakely, Richard Chamberlain, Jennifer Jones, O.J. Simpson.

61. NETWORK. MGM, 1976 (c). *Sidney Lumet*. Sp: Paddy Chayefsky. Cast: Faye Dunaway, Peter Finch, Robert Duvall, Darryl Hickman, Conchata Ferrell.

62. 21 HOURS AT MUNICH. Filmways, 1977 (c). *William A. Graham*. Sp: Edward Hume and E. V. Cunningham. Cast: Shirley Knight, Franco Nero.

Holden also appeared in two short films: *Wings Up* (1943), a recruiting film for the Army Air Corps, narrated by Clark Gable and also featuring Gilbert Roland, Robert Preston, and Brenda Marshall, and *You Can Change the World* (1950), a film for the Christophers, directed by Leo McCarey.

INDEX

Addams, Dawn, 96
Adler, Luther, 25, 28
African Queen, The, 119
All About Eve, 79
All the King's Men, 82
Allen, Irwin, 143
Alvarez Kelly, 132-133, 135
Apartment for Peggy, 64
Arizona, 39-40, 44
Arnold, Edward, 59, 71
Arthur, Jean, 40
Axelrod, George, 130

Bacon, Lloyd, 69
Bainter, Fay, 37
Ball, Lucille, 69
Ballard, Lucien, 139
Balzac, Honoré, 73
Barrett, Judith, 39
Barrie, J. M., 100
Baxter, Anne, 59
Baxter, Warner, 106
Beedle, Bob, 16, 54, 112
Beedle, Mary Bell, 16, 19, 28, 48
Beedle, Richard, 16
Beedle, William Franklin, Sr., 16, 19
Begley, Ed, 88
Bellamy, Ralph, 65
Ben Ali, Bob, 20
Benchley, Robert, 52
Bendix, William, 59, 67, 68
Bettger, Lyle, 82
Bevan, Donald, 88
Blaze of Noon, 58-59, 87
Blind Alley, 65
Blue Knight, The, 144
Blum, Edwin, 88
Boehm, Sydney, 82
Bogart, Humphrey, 35, 104, 106
Bondi, Beulah, 37
Boots Malone, 87
Born Yesterday, 82-86
Boulle, Pierre, 117, 119, 120
Bourgoin, Jean, 127
Bracken, Eddie, 51, 52

Brackett, Charles, 73, 76
Brand, Neville, 92
Breezy, 142, 143
Bridge on the River Kwai, The, 117-120, 121
Bridge Over the River Kwai, The (novel), 117
Bridges at Toko-Ri, The, 108-110, 112
Britton, Barbara, 52
Brophy, Edward, 32
Brown, Gilmore, 22
Buchanan, Edgar, 44

Calhern, Louis, 103
Calleia, Joseph, 32
Capra, Frank, 48
Capucine, 129, 131, 132
Cardiff, Jack, 129
Carey, Macdonald, 67
Casino Royale, 135
Caulfield, Joan, 61, 71, 72
Chandlee, Harry, 37
Chayefsky, Paddy, 143n
Christmas Tree, The, 139, 141
Clark, Kenneth, 86
Clift, Montgomery, 75
Clothier, William, 122
Clurman, Harold, 28
Cobb, Lee J., 25, 30, 67
Cohn, Harry, 25, 26, 27, 28, 30, 39
Cooper, Gary, 39, 61
Copeland, Aaron, 37
Counterfeit Traitor, The, 127, 129
Country Girl, The, 106-108
Crain, Jeanne, 64
Craven, Frank, 37
Crawford, Broderick, 82, 85
Crosby, Bing, 61, 106, 108
Crowley, Pat, 100
Cukor, George, 82
Curtiz, Michael, 87
Cyrano de Bergerac, 79

da Sylva, Howard, 59
Dark Past, The, 64-65, 67
de Hartog, Jan, 121

155

De Lapp, Terry, 24
De Wolfe, Billy, 59
Dear Brat, 72
Dear Ruth, 56, 59, 61, 71
Dear Wife, 71-72
Destry Rides Again, 44
Devil's Brigade, The, 135, 137
Dieterle, William, 87
Dirty Dozen, The, 135
Dmytryk, Edward, 133
Donlevy, Brian, 44, 47, 48
Douglas, Paul, 85, 100
Drew, Ellen, 24, 48
Dunaway, Faye, 143n
Dunn, Elizabeth, 51
Dyer, Elmer, 42

Eastwood, Clint, 142
Edwards, Blake, 141
Epstein, Julius, 100
Epstein, Phillip, 100
Erdman, Richard, 92
Erickson, Eric, 127
Escape From Fort Bravo, 100
Executive Suite, 100, 103-104

Fain, Sammy, 112
Farrow, John, 58, 87
Father is a Bachelor, 72
Feldman, Charles K., 135
Fenton, Leslie, 67
Ferrer, Jose, 79
Field, Betty, 24, 115
Finch, Peter, 143n
Fitch, George, 37
Fitzgerald, Barry, 82
Fleet's In, The, 48, 51
Flynn, Errol, 47

Force of Arms, 87
Ford, Glenn, 44, 67
Ford, John, 39, 122, 123, 135
Foreman, Carl, 121
Forever Female, 100
42nd Street, 106
Foster, Norman, 63
Franklin, Pamela, 129
Frawley, William, 39
Freeman, Devery, 69
Freeman, Mona, 59, 67, 68, 71, 72

Gable, Clark, 55
Gaines, Richard Huston, 47
Garfield, John, 25
Gehman, Richard, 56
Gibson, Althea, 123
Gibson, Hoot, 123
Going My Way, 124
Golden Boy, 11, 25-34, 42, 67, 104, 144
Golden Boy (stage), 20
Gone With the Wind, 30
Good Ole Siwash, 37
Grant, Cary, 42, 104, 130
Granville, Bonita, 39
Graves, Peter, 92, 94
Griffith, Edward, 53
Guinness, Alec, 120

Hatari!, 129
Hatcher, Mary, 61
Hawks, Howard, 58, 129
Hawley, Cameron, 103
Hayakawa, Sessue, 120
Hayden, Sterling, 59
Hayward, Susan, 24, 52, 142
Heesters, Johannes, 96
Hepburn, Audrey, 99, 104, 106, 130

Herbert, F. Hugh, 96
Heston, Charlton, 92
Holden, Ardis (Brenda Marshall), 47, 54, 55, 56, 144
Holden, Peter, 54
Holden, Scott, 56, 142
Holden, Virginia, 47
Holden, William (*Los Angeles Times*), 24
Holiday For Henrietta, 130
Holliday, Judy, 82, 85
Hope, Bob, 61
Horse Soldiers, The, 122, 135
Howe, James Wong, 113
Hutton, Betty, 51

I Wanted Wings, 40, 42, 44
Informer, The, 135
Inge, William, 112, 113
Invisible Stripes, 35, 44

Jagger, Dean, 103
Johnson, Artie, 22
Jones, Jennifer, 112
Jones, Spike, 61
Jungfrau Auf Dem Dach, Die (The Moon is Blue), 99

Kanin, Garson, 82
Kazan, Elia, 32
Kefauver, Estes, 88
Keller, Father James, 86
Kelly, Grace, 106, 108
Kerr, Deborah, 115
Key, The, 121-122
Kibbee, Guy, 37
King, Henry, 112
Kingdom of God, The, 112
Krasna, Norman, 59

Kruger, Hardy, 96
Kwan, Nancy, 124

Ladd, Alan, 56, 61
Lake, Veronica, 42, 44
Lamour, Dorothy, 51
Lang, Charles, Jr., 106
Lawes, Lewis E., 35
Leisen, Mitchell, 42
Lembeck, Harvey, 92, 94
Lenz, Kay, 142
Lesser, Sol, 37
Levene, Sam, 25, 32
Lewis, Milton, 22
Lion, The, 129
Logan, Joshua, 112, 113
Lombardo, Louis, 138
Loren, Sophia, 121
Love is a Many-Splendored Thing, 112

MacMichael, Florence, 52
MacMullan, Hugh, 29, 44
McCarey, Leo, 86, 124, 125
McCrea, Joel, 39
McHugh, Frank, 71
McLaglen, Andrew, 135, 137
McLaglen, Victor, 135
McNamara, Maggie, 96, 97, 99
Mamoulian, Rouben, 25, 26, 27, 28, 30, 32
Man From Colorado, The, 67
Manhandled, 75
Mankiewicz, Joseph L., 79
Mann, Daniel, 142
Manya, 20, 22
March, Fredric, 103, 104, 110
Marshall, Brenda (Ardis Holden), 47, 54, 55, 56, 144
Marshall, George, 44

Marshman, D. M., 73
Maté, Rudolph, 64, 65, 82
Matz, Johanna, 96
Meeker, Ralph, 112
Meet The Stewarts, 48, 51
Menjou, Adolphe, 25, 30
Menzies, William Cameron, 37
Merrill, Gary, 85
Merry Widow, The, 97
Michener, James, 108
Milland, Ray, 40, 42, 61
Million Dollar Legs, 24
Miracle on 34th Street, 64
Miss Grant Takes Richmond, 69, 71
Mr. Smith Goes to Washington, 30
Mitchell, Thomas, 37
Mitchum, Robert, 63
Moon is Blue, The, 96-100
Moore, Constance, 42
Mooring, William H., 86
Morris, Chester, 65
Morris, Wayne, 40, 42

Network, 143n
Niven, David, 96, 97
Nolan, Lloyd, 115
Novak, Kim, 115
Novelli, Carla, 135
Novelli, Giorgio, 135
Nuyen, France, 125

O'Brien, Edmond, 88
O'Connell, Arthur, 113
O'Driscoll, Martha, 52
O'Neal, Ryan, 141
Odets, Clifford, 20, 25, 28, 32, 106
Olson, Nancy, 76, 82, 87
On the Waterfront, 119

Only Angels Have Wings, 58
Open Season, 143
Out of the Frying Pan, 52

Paris When it Sizzles, 130
Parker, Eleanor, 100
Peckinpah, Sam, 137, 138
Père Goriot, Le, 73
Perlberg, William, 27
Perrin, Nat, 69
Philips, Mary, 59
Picnic, 11, 112-113, 115
Pidgeon, Walter, 103
Pierson, William, 92
Preminger, Otto, 92, 94, 96, 99, 100
Preston, Robert, 24, 55
Prison Farm, 24
Proud and the Profane, The, 115

Queen Kelly, 76

Rachel and the Stranger, 61-64
Raft, George, 35
Rapper, Irving, 100
Razor's Edge, The, 59
Reed, Sir Carol, 121
Remarkable Andrew, The, 47-48
Revengers, The, 142
Rip Van Winkle, 16
Robertson, Cliff, 113
Robson, Mark, 110
Rogers, Ginger, 100
Roland, Gilbert, 55
Rooney, Mickey, 110
Rosalind, 100
Ruggles, Wesley, 39, 40
Ruman, Sig, 94
Russell, Rosalind, 113

Sabrina, 104-106
Sabrina Fair, 104
Sailor Beware, 48
Salt, Waldo, 63
Satan Never Sleeps, 123, 124-125
San Juan, Olga, 61
Scott, Martha, 37
Sea Hawk, The, 47
Seaton, George, 64, 106, 115, 127
Seventh Dawn, The, 131-132
Sheekman, Arthur, 59
Siegel, Sol C., 135
Smith, Alexis, 88
Spiegel, Sam, 119
Stagecoach, 30, 39
Stalag 17, 11, 88-95, 96
Stanwyck, Barbara, 25, 30, 32, 34, 61, 103, 104
Star-Spangled Rhythm, 61
Stone, Ezra, 39
Strasberg, Susan, 115
Stratton, Gil, Jr., 94
Strauss, Robert, 92, 94
Streets of Laredo, 67-69
Sturges, John, 100
Submarine Command, 87
Sunset Boulevard, 11, 73-79, 82
Suyin, Han, 112
Swann, Francis, 52
Swanson, Gloria, 75, 76, 85

Tashlin, Frank, 69
Taylor, Don, 92
Taylor, Samuel, 104
Texas, 44
Thompson, Francis, 112
Those Were the Days, 37, 39
Toward the Unknown, 115-116

Towering Inferno, The, 143
Trevor, Claire, 44
Trumbo, Dalton, 47, 48
Trzcinski, Edmund, 88, 92
Tufts, Sonny, 59
Turning Point, The, 87-88

Union Station, 82

Variety Girl, 61
von Stroheim, Erich, 76

Wambaugh, Joseph, 144
Warner, Jack, 25
Wasson, Rebecca, 22, 27
Wayne, John, 122, 123, 125
Wead, Frank, 58
Webb, Clifton, 124
Weiler, A. H., 67
Whispering Smith, 56
Widmark, Richard, 133
Wild Bunch, The, 137-139, 141
Wild Rovers, 141-142
Wilder, Billy, 73, 75, 76, 79, 81, 88, 92, 94, 95, 104, 106, 112
Wilder, Thornton, 35, 37
William Holden's Untamed World, 144
Wings Up, 55
Wise, Robert, 103
Wizard of Oz, The, 30
Wolper, Dave, 144
Wood, Sam, 37
World of Suzie Wong, The, 123-124

You Can Change the World, 86
Young and Willing, 51-53, 142
Young, Carleton, 123
Young, Loretta, 63
Young, Terence, 139

ABOUT THE AUTHOR
Will Holtzman has lectured on film at Wesleyan University, in Middletown, Connecticut and has written for the *Real Paper, The Journal of Popular Film*, and the Film Department of the Hartford Atheneum. He is a regular contributor to the Book Section of the *St. Louis Globe-Democrat*.

ABOUT THE EDITOR
Ted Sennett is the author of *Warner Brothers Presents*, a tribute to the great Warners films of the thirties and forties, and of *Lunatics and Lovers*, on the long-vanished but well-remembered "screwball" movies of the past. He is also the editor of *The Movie Buff's Book* and has written about films for magazines and newspapers. He lives in New Jersey with his wife and three children.